Marriage Management

Molly,
Thank you so much for your
help with this project!
Being a Grammar Nazi is
a blessing!

— Tim

Marriage Management

A Practical Approach to Marital Fulfillment

Tim Russo

ISBN-13: 9781467951272
ISBN-10: 1467951277
Library of Congress Control Number: 2016903145
CreateSpace Independent Publishing Platform
North Charleston, South Carolina

Contents

Endorsements

"Tim Russo has an unshakeable passion for Godly marriages. My confidence in Tim is such that I have invited him to present his *Marriage Management* material to one of my classes. The members of that class asked me to have him back for another infusion of his wisdom. I am sure that you will find this book to be very useful!"

- Jon R Anderson, Founder of Growing Love Network and author of
Growing Love and 365 Days of Growing Love

The timeless maxim "an ounce of prevention is worth a pound of cure" is familiar to us all. In the context of marriage, we're all aware that every marriage needs intentional effort, planning, and attention. But how? Too often, the way forward seems cloudy at best and cryptic at worst. In his new book, Marriage Management, Tim Russo lays out a clear path forward and attaches his ideas to a concept that we're thoroughly familiar with. The book shares the marriage wisdom of a pastor and counselor alongside a strategic plan for implementation - it is rich with meaning but also intensely practical in application. I have the highest regard for Tim and I'm excited to consider how many couples can use this marriage manual in growing toward a stronger and vibrant marriage.

- Carl Caton, Founder of San Antonio Marriage Initiative

Tim Russo's "Marriage Management" is a rare blend of defining marriage in the highest, most eternal contexts. Tim's use of financial management terminology is a unique way to connect us to what we know and understand well: investment, income, expenses, debt. His emphasis on commitment and work communicates undeniably that no strong marriage happens by accident. It is extremely helpful to have a book like "Marriage Management" to encourage and guide our steps. Read this book and you will applaud Tim Russo for his valuable voice and insights to our marriages.

- Dave Galbraith, Founder of *Breakthrough Moments*

Acknowledgements

Few things have impacted my life the way being married has. I was 20 years young when I said "I Do" to God, Elaine and a church full of family and friends. Little did I know then how powerfully those two little words would impact my life! Like so many young men, I had a very limited understanding of what it meant to be a husband, to take on the responsibility of leading a family, and to love another person as Christ loved the church.

This book is dedicated to:

- My dear wife who has been my constant companion, dearest friend, fellow learner, and the greatest human example I've known of what it means to love and serve others authentically, graciously, and compassionately.
- my daughters, sons-in-law, and grandchildren, all of whom have been used by God to shape me into the person I am today.
- my dear friends who have stood with us through many years of ministry and to whom I owe a great deal of gratitude.
- to husbands who need encouragement and inspiration.
- most importantly, to the Lord Jesus, who rescued my life from utter destruction and blessed me in more ways than I am aware.

Preface

As we begin, it is probably beneficial to say a few things about marriage in general. Marriage is God's institution (Gen. 3). It is not a human arrangement for human benefit (although there are certainly benefits for those who embrace it). Rather, marriage was designed for God's purpose. He established the marriage relationship before any other, and it is intended to reflect His character in a special way (Eph. 5:32). For example, when we display things like love, patience, sacrifice, forgiveness, kindness, and graciousness, those observing our marriage see a reflection of God's character. Thus, a sense of hope is created or revived, especially for those who have struggled in their marriage. Two other characteristics reflect God's image, unity and peace. The Bible instructs us to work hard at guarding and keeping this unity and peace (Eph. 4:1). This implies that unity and peace are fragile and can be easily neglected and even destroyed.

If reflecting God's character is a primary purpose of marriage, it is reasonable to expect many obstacles along the journey. Some of these obstacles come from life circumstances. Others come from within our own hearts. In fact, most of the obstacles married couples will face are directly related to personal desires and expectations.

It is important for us to see the bigger picture in which our lives and marriages play a small part. Marriage is primarily for God's glory and pleasure. Although marriage is not designed primarily to make us happy, when we follow God's blueprints, we find happiness and contentment. However, when we mistakenly assume that being married (or our spouse) will make us happy, we enter dangerous territory and end up, like so many couples, misusing marriage for purposes for which it was never designed.

The purpose of this book is to help you, as individuals and as a couple, better manage your marriage relationship. In a very real sense, we are stewards of the marriage covenant. As stewards, we must seek to be found faithful (1 Cor. 4:2).

I have observed three general categories of people regarding God's blueprints for marriage: 1. Those who have never heard or considered what God has to say about marriage in general or their marriage specifically. This book is not intended to address God's blueprints. 2. Those who have heard what God has to say about marriage but struggle to apply these concepts to real life. Subsequently, they become discouraged when they do not experience the abundance God intended. 3. Those who know and apply God's blueprints for marriage and subsequently experience, to one degree or another, what He intended.

This book is directed toward category 2—those who have heard what God has to say about marriage but for whatever reasons, fail to experience what God intends for them as married couples.

Most of the couples I meet with in counseling are aware of the "what" of marriage (what they should or should not be doing). However, they struggle with the "how." Although this book is not capable of, nor intended to, address the full scope of applying God's principles to life and marriage, it is intended to give a broad picture and introduce you to the concept of Marriage Management.

Throughout this book, you will be asked to complete a portion of the *Marriage Budget Worksheet* (Individual version). You will complete each of the four categories (which I will explain in detail) on your own without your spouse's involvement. After you have completed your Individual *Marriage Budge Worksheet*, you and your spouse will compare your items in each category. Then, together, you will come up with your unique *Marriage Budget* which you both can agree on. If you need additional copies of the *Marriage Budget Worksheet*, you can download it from http://relationalimpact.com.

Disclaimer: The stories and examples I share in the book are real life example. However, the names have been changed.

Introduction

have yet to meet a man or woman who planned to fail at marriage. We enter marriage with optimistic hopes and dreams. Our intentions are admirable. We exit the wedding ceremony smiling and excited about the future.

Before long we are faced with obstacles which demand our attention and which, if not handled properly, can quickly deplete our emotional resources.

Through my years of working with couples, I have seen the all-too-common look of confusion on the face of a perplexed husband or wife after hitting the proverbial brick wall in their relationship. That look is familiar to me because I have experienced confusion more times than I'd like to admit. The same vows I made so eagerly on our wedding day later filled me with an overwhelming sense of inadequacy. "*Will you love her and cherish her?*" I eagerly said "*I will,*" but did I really understand what love was? Was I aware that loving and cherishing Elaine would require me changing, growing, and sacrificing? Did I realize that to love Elaine meant putting Elaine's needs above mine? A firm "No" to all the above. Neither did I realize how much I would need God and His resources to love her the way He loves her.

Thankfully, I have learned a few things about what it means to be a husband. Yet it seems like every time I become comfortable in one season of life, the season changes, and I become aware that there is much more to learn and many more ways to express love.

Like many husbands, I struggled being the spiritual leader in our home. In the early years of our marriage, lots of books and messages were becoming available on the subject of being a husband and father. At first, this new information was exciting; it motivated me to be a better husband. Yet after many failed attempts, I became discouraged, and the information which once motivated me became a constant reminder of my failures. I knew "what" I should be doing (I even taught it to our congregation), but I struggled with the "how."

I felt the frustration of what the Apostle Paul wrote to the Romans: *to will is present with me, but how to perform what is good I do not find* (Rom. 7:18). I felt like I was under a huge burden, a looming threat of failure. Try as I might, I could not get on top of the problem. I was confused. I seemed to be able to learn and grow in other areas of my life, yet when it came to being a husband, I felt clueless and lost. As a result, I became a more passive husband. I found myself avoiding conversations with Elaine. In short, I chose not to engage.

But God answers prayers! He knew I needed to come to the end of myself, along with my resources and abilities. I would need to rely completely upon Him. I am a visual learner; I learn and understand concepts better when I can see them either on paper or in my mind's eye. I had benefitted from the popular concepts of the "Love Bank" or "Love Tank," (Harley, Smalley, Chapman). According to this concept, a husband can make deposits into his wife's love bank through positive gestures, etc. He makes withdrawals by negative contributions to the relationship. Thus, if a husband makes more withdrawals than deposits, the relationship will eventually go bankrupt.

This concept gave me a fresh desire to work at being a better husband. The most encouraging part about the Love Bank concept was that I now had *a plan!* Instead of the "hope you get it right" approach, I became more intentional about my words and actions toward Elaine.

The concept of making deposits and withdrawals was the beginning of what has become known as *The Marriage Budget.* I began to view my marriage as a stewardship. I began to understand that the marriage covenant, which Elaine and I entered into, belonged to God. He designed it. He created it. He owns the copyright. When Elaine and I entered into His covenant, we became responsible for the stewardship of it.

The Marriage Budget is a simple way of seeing your marriage on paper. It helps to put things into perspective. It gives us tracks to run on, practical ways of understanding and applying the Biblical concepts of marriage and relationships in general.

By viewing marriage practically--logically--I was able to see more clearly *how* to put into practice the information I had learned through the years. I was no longer intimidated by the expectations and duties marriage required. *The Marriage Budget* helped me become a better manager of my marriage.

My hope is that this simple concept of *Marriage Management* will help free you to be all you were meant to be, to find enjoyment and fulfillment in being married, and to help you have the best marriage possible.

Note: Although I believe these concepts can be equally beneficial to men and women, I have chosen to write with a male audience in view. Thus, my comments will highlight how men can become proactive and intentional about managing their marriages.

Chapter 1
The Big Picture

Building Principles

B efore we get into the details of the *Marriage Budget*, it may be helpful to see the 30,000-foot view of the development process of marriage--the big picture. When I am embarking on a new journey, it helps me to know my long-term objective. I need answers to questions like, "What are we doing? What's the point?" Once I know this, I have a much better chance of moving toward the objective.

The Biblical passage that lays out building plans more clearly than any other is Proverbs 24:3-4. When it comes to Biblical principles for building, the writer of Proverbs gives us a clear picture of what to expect. Although our specific topic is marriage, the principles found in this passage apply to any building venture. Whether you are building a family, a business, a school, or a church, these Biblical principles apply.

Through wisdom a house is built, by understanding it is established, by knowledge the rooms are filled with all precious and pleasant riches (Proverbs 24:3-4).

The chart below illustrates three phases which every building endeavor must go through.

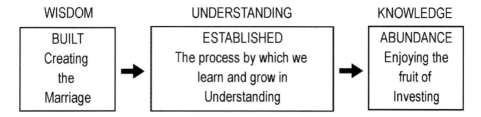

WISDOM	UNDERSTANDING	KNOWLEDGE
BUILT	ESTABLISHED	ABUNDANCE
Creating the Marriage	The process by which we learn and grow in Understanding	Enjoying the fruit of Investing

A Beginning

The first of the three phases in the building process is to build or begin. (*Through wisdom a house* [family] *is built*). The word *build* in this verse means to *have a beginning*. The same word is used in the book of Genesis where we read that God took a rib from Adam and *made* (built) Eve (Gen. 2:22). Noah *built* an Ark (Gen. 8:20). In the context of marriage, *to build* would mean to get married--say "I Do!" It is in this phase that you take the necessary steps to create the institution. It is your starting point. For most couples, the beginning phase of the building process is actually the easiest (although it can be very expensive). The Proverb states that this step requires *wisdom*. Wisdom is the application of knowledge. It is doing what you know needs to be done. A wise person takes God at His Word and does what He instructs. This implies that an element of faith is required.

For others, this step is excruciating. The fear attached to making such a huge commitment is staggering for many young people today, especially young men. More and more couples are choosing to avoid this all important *building* phase of marriage because they want to make sure the relationship is right. I won't spend time on this point. Authors such as Tim Keller, Shaunti Feldhahn, and others have done a great job explaining the psychology and science behind this phenomenon.[1][2]

When a couple avoids the beginning phase of commitment to marriage, they risk never being able to experience the other phases of the building process. There must be a beginning. For most, this phase is filled with excitement and anticipation.

Establishing Phase

The second phase of building can be the longest and most difficult. This is the phase in which some give up on their marriage. A business consultant tried to encourage a man who gave up on his business endeavor after six months by telling him, "It takes three years to build a business." Most successful business owners would agree that it takes between 3 and 5 years for a business to become established and successful. Many new hopeful entrepreneurs have placed a new sign on their building or launched their very well-put-together website, only to become discouraged when customers did not come to their businesses by the hundreds. Perhaps their expectations were misplaced. Perhaps they believed, like many newlyweds, that simply starting the entity would be enough. Many of these potential entrepreneurs failed to realize the amount of work it takes to establish their dream business.

The challenges and obstacles involved in establishing a marriage can sometimes seem overwhelming. Yet facing and overcoming these obstacles is necessary. Just like the butterfly's struggle to escape its cocoon strengthens and enables him to fly, a couple's struggle to make adjustments in the face of difficulties, and work as a team strengthens them and enables them to experience fulfillment in their marriage.

The Proverb states that understanding is necessary for establishing a family (*by understanding it is established*). If it takes 3 to 5 years to establish a business, should we expect anything less of marriage? Some research shows that most divorces occur during the first five years of marriage (Kreider, 2005).[3] I have met with several couples, married only one year or less, who were considering divorce. Because these couples were having conflicts more frequently, they viewed this as a reason to contemplate divorce. They did not expect to have a high degree of conflict. The more they argued, the more they began to think they married the wrong person. Their expectations (mostly unrealistic) were dashed, and now disappointment and discouragement set in.

What would happen if young couples expected conflict? What if they were prepared to argue constructively? What if, when they hit the proverbial brick wall in their relationship, they said, "Oh, this is what people told us would happen. We must be normal!"

When a couple expects difficulty; when they understand that God uses conflict to mature them; when they realize that every successful marriage experiences similar obstacles; when they accept that the difficulties they face are normal; when they are committed to staying loyal to each other, God, and their marriage vows, they will be in a much better position to establish a strong and lasting marriage.

Without *understanding*, a couple will be susceptible to unnecessary temptation to abort the process of establishing their marriage. We need to grow in our understanding of God's purpose for marriage. Part of that growth process includes growing in our understanding of one another's strengths and weaknesses. This will contribute to a stronger, more established marriage.

The verses below are examples of the Bible's emphasis on understanding:

A wise man will hear and increase learning, and a man of understanding will attain wise counsel (Proverbs 1:5).

Discretion will preserve you; understanding will keep you (Proverbs 2:11).

He who gets wisdom loves his own soul; he who keeps understanding will find good (Proverbs 19:8).

The *establishing* phase allows a couple to make adjustments and embrace important and necessary changes in their relationship dynamics. They will learn to adapt to each other's unique differences and grow in love.

As you and your spouse persevere through the establishing phase of building your marriage, you will begin experiencing the benefits of your investments. You will have weathered many storms together and learned to communicate and love much better than you did in the beginning of your relationship. Your relationship will be established and growing.

Abundance Phase

The Secret to fulfillment is adding value to others.

The abundance phase is where we begin to reap the rewards of our investments. It is also in this phase that we learn to apply the secret of fulfillment: *adding value to others.* Adding value to others is the most powerful and productive choice you and I can make.

The abundance phase is what newly married couples anticipate when they marry. It is the *preciousness and pleasantness* of walking through life with your companion and friend. Those who have gone through the establishing phase find unexpected rewards of abundance. As the Proverbs states, their relationship is *filled with all precious and pleasant riches.* It is the reward of persevering through difficult times and remaining faithful to God and to each other.

Although this phase is not problem-free, the investments made in years past have now produced a reservoir of resources that continually provide you and your spouse with strength to face every situation. The things you grew in, such as love, peace, joy, contentment and patience, have now become permanent fixtures – qualities – in your relationship. Your appreciation for each other has risen to a height that causes others to notice. Your marriage reflects God's image!

A Lesson from My Lawn

When our family moved into our new home in West Texas, the front lawn was covered with Puncturevine, otherwise known by locals as *Goatheads*. If you have ever stepped on a goathead without shoes, you know how horrifying these little monsters are! Anyway, I wanted to get rid of these horrible stickers because we could not enjoy our lawn. Also, when friends came to visit, some unknowingly walked in the lawn and got a surprising fright! They also brought the little stickers into the front room of the house. I decided it was time to fix this problem. I went to our local lawn and garden store to buy whatever powerful chemical I needed to get rid of these weaponized plants. To my surprise, the lawn care expert told me there was no way to get rid of the goatheads by trying to kill them. He explained the correct process. First, you must fertilize your lawn and water it regularly for a month or so. As your lawn becomes healthy, the good grass will crowd out the goatheads. Then, you simply spot treat the ones that remain and you'll be done. Your problem will be solved.

Who knew? There I was, thinking I needed to focus on the goatheads (of course they were the object of my anger, the ultimate spur under my saddle, when all along, I needed to work on getting my lawn healthy.

I have thought about this lesson from my lawn many times since that day. When we focus on getting rid of our marriage problems, we will be fighting a losing battle. The secret is to understand the growth process and to direct our efforts toward adding to our marital resources.

The Marriage Budget

The *Marriage Management* is a way to be intentional about the condition of your marriage. Like a financial budget, the *Marriage Budget* is a tool to help you manage your marital resources. It's a way of tracking what is taking place in your relationship.

Managing your marriage starts with an accurate assessment. You can do this by asking and eventually answering three basic questions:

1. Where are we currently? (What is our current marital picture? How are we doing?)
2. Where do we desire to be? (A better question may be, "Where does God want us to be?)
3. How will we get there? (What is the plan?)

God gave pertinent instructions to the prophet Haggai, which may be helpful to us:

> *Consider your ways. You have sown much and bring in little. You eat, but do not have enough. You drink, but you are not filled with drink. You clothe yourselves, but no one is warm. And he who earns wages, earns wages to put into a bag with holes. Thus says the Lord, consider your ways.* (Haggai 1:5-7)

The *Marriage Budget* is a tool to help you consider your marital ways (habits). Instead of just letting your relationship happen naturally, you become a steward of your marriage.

The *Marriage Budget* consists of four basic categories:

- Income Sources
- Expenses (necessary and unnecessary)
- Debt (unresolved issues)
- Investments (Giving)

Let's take a look at each category.

Chapter 2

Income Sources

An Income Source is something that requires effort and adds to your relationship. An Income Source can be something done by one spouse for the other or something done as a couple.

Three Connecting Points

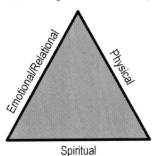

Connecting Points for Intimacy

I want to suggest that there are three primary areas for connecting in your relationship. 1) *Relational* (includes the emotional). This area includes spending time together, having fun, enjoying friends and activities, conversation, etc. 2) *Physical*. This area includes both sexual and non-sexual connecting (holding hands, a gentle touch on the shoulder, etc.) 3) *Spiritual*. Couples who share the same faith and theological views have more freedom to connect spiritually. However, any couple can benefit from having conversations about their faith and how relative God is to them and their life. As you begin to identify Income Sources for your marriage, these connecting points can serve as a guide.

It is not uncommon for a couple to connect in one area of their relationship but struggle in another. For example, you may do very well connecting as friends in the relationship/emotional category, but have very little or no connection in the spiritual category. Another couple may have a strong spiritual connection but have little or no connection when it comes to their physical relationship. Or a couple may be great friends and enjoy each other's company, but their sexual relationship is weak.

As we explore the subject of *Marriage Management* and working through *Marriage Budget*, it will be helpful for you to keep these three connecting points in mind. Let's take a look at some common Income Sources.

Income Sources

Income Sources strengthen your relationship. An Income Source may be an attitude of respect, a gesture of appreciation, or an unexpected gift; it is anything positive that adds to your relationship.

Enough studies have been done to identify certain components that contribute to building a strong marriage. These attitudes and actions are predictable in generating positive Income for a couple. One of the most essential Income Sources is *good communication*. This includes speaking the truth in love, sharing your thoughts, feelings, and opinions, learning good problem-solving and conflict resolution skills, and learning active listening habits.

Other simple gestures like showing non-verbal affection (a smile, or a wink across the room) can be powerful Income Sources for your marriage. Surprisingly, even a little effort can produce a good amount of income in a relationship. When a husband gives his wife a rose (or a dozen roses), his thoughtful gesture can have a huge impact on his wife, and thus, his marriage.

Some people are not sure of what would be considered Income for their life or marriage. You may need some ideas to get started. If you need to better understand Income Sources, continue reading. I have listed a few of the more common things that seem to bring couples Income. Through the years, I have identified 3 types of couples: 1) *Don't have any*. These couples have neglected their relationship to the point that they don't do anything to add to their relationship. They exist in the same family, but are like ships passing in the night, rarely interacting or sharing experiences. 2) *Didn't know they were called Income Sources.* These couples certainly have Income Sources for their marriage but they have never given them such a name. For these couples, listing Income Sources will be easier. They will simply list what they already do. 3) *Yes we do!* These couples are intentional about building their relationship. They are aware of what it takes to keep their marriage strong. For these, creating a marriage budget is a simple process of cataloging the components of their growing relationship.

Common Income Sources
Prayer

The habit of prayer is a great discipline for couples and one that can help strengthen your spiritual connection. However, praying together can be a difficult task and sometimes awkward. A number of factors may contribute to this. It could be as simple as a husband or wife not being accustomed to praying at all, especially aloud where another person can hear. It may be an unresolved conflict residing under the surface. It could be anger or feeling misunderstood. You may feel unaccepted or disrespected; one or both feel unsafe and don't want to be vulnerable. It is very easy to allow obstacles like these to hinder you from praying together as a couple. These obstacles convince us that it's too much work. However, if you will commit to praying together, regardless of the circumstances, you will see tremendous benefits. If this is a new idea, start with 2 or 3 minutes, thanking God for His blessings in your life. Remember, little changes can bring major benefit. I have listed a few resources in the back of the book that might be helpful in this area. [4]

Life-Long Commitment

> *...what God has joined together, let not man separate* (Matt. 19:6).

Elaine and I married young. We had so much to learn. However, early on, we agreed that we would never use the word "divorce" in reference to us; it would never be an option. This decision enabled us to weather the many storms our relationship would eventually experience.

Being committed to a lifetime together provides a relationship with a strong foundation for building a lasting marriage. Staying loyal to your marriage vows, living together until death separates you, provides a relational environment for change and growth. God intends for your marriage to last a lifetime, until one of you dies. He knows very well what your personal and marital needs are. He also knows there will be times you are tempted to quit and give up. Your commitment to persevere through the inevitable and necessary hard times of life will facilitate the development of your personal character (Jam. 1:2-5; 1 Pet. 1:6), thereby reflecting the God in whom you trust.

Marriage and family life is the laboratory for character development. Conflicts and challenges provide an environment to realize our great need for God and change. It helps us see our need to embrace God's ways rather than ours. The wise man, Solomon, wrote: *The refining pot is for silver and the furnace for gold, but the LORD tests the hearts* (Prov. 17:3). Your commitment to God and your spouse provides a safe environment for personal and marital growth. If you doubt whether your spouse is committed to you, you will likely not make yourself vulnerable and transparent. You will be guarded so as to protect yourself. The marriage covenant is intended to provide that safe environment.

In our *BluePrints for Marriage* Seminar, we encourage couples to renew their marriage vows. The reason is simple: many couples, when they originally recited their vows, did not fully comprehend the importance of those words.

Your commitment to your spouse must be unwavering. She must know that for better or worse, richer or poor, sickness or in health, you are there to stay! With this foundation, you will be able to build a strong marriage that will endure every marital storm.

Good Habits

God designed us as creatures of habit. Most of what we do in a given day is done almost effortlessly through habits. Habit is automatic and unconscious behavior. Anything, from the simple task of brushing your teeth to the complicated task of driving an automobile, is all done through the brilliant invention of habit. The great thing about habits is that once intentional behavior becomes a habit, you will do it automatically. By developing good habits, you will consistently contribute to your growing relationship.

Personal Growth

Commit to a life of learning--a life of growing, changing, and pursuing the Lord. If you are a Believer, the Lord is in the process of conforming you to His image (Romans 8:29). He doesn't do this work without your cooperation. You must participate in the conforming process by responding to Him and His Word. The more like Him you become, the better you will reflect His grace at work in you, enabling you to better love your spouse and others. Life happens in seasons (Ps. 1:3; Ecc. 3:1). Through every season of life, you will encounter new life lessons. God gives time and seasons for specific purposes. It is important to give each other room to grow through these seasons of change. When a wife becomes a new mother, her priorities may change. One wife thought she would certainly be in the workplace and help reach her and her husband's financial goals. They had discussed it early in their relationship. Yet when she held her newborn in her arms, she knew she would not be able to leave him. This is but one example of how the seasons of life create opportunities to learn and grow.

The couple who is flexible will respond better to unexpected circumstances. Be aware that God may have something planned for your marriage and family that you have not anticipated. Being committed to personal growth can be a huge benefit to your marriage in these cases.

Good Communication

Communication is to marriage what skating is to ice hockey.

There are many good books on the topic of communication[5] so I won't spend a lot to time here. However, a few things are worth mentioning. Communication is to marriage what skating is to ice hockey. If a player does not know how to skate, he will not play the game well. He certainly will never enjoy it. Only when skilled skating becomes a habit can the player really focus on the game of hockey.

The same is true for communication in marriage. If you have not learned how to skillfully communicate with your spouse, you will struggle in your marriage. As in the game of Hockey, you certainly will not enjoy it. You will stumble as soon as you get on the ice. For a lot of men, the problem intensifies when our wives are good communicators and we struggle.

When couples employ good communication, they are able to successfully navigate through any situation that arises. When a couple is weak in communication, even the smallest problem goes unresolved, and it is added to the pile of unresolved issues. In the spirit of the popular saying, "Teach a man to fish and you feed him for a lifetime," teach a couple to communicate and you enable them to successfully navigate anything they encounter.

Elaine and I have had our struggles because of poor communication. Elaine comes from a background of honest and forthright communication. I, on the other hand, learned to communicate in code. You never really said exactly what you meant. You said something (in code), and the other person was to decode the message; you know, they should read between the lines. As you might imagine, it did not take long for our communication styles to clash. Elaine would say something that was on her mind and I would try to decode what she said. The problem was, she had just said exactly what she meant! This took some adjusting to, to say the least.

My struggle intensified when Elaine wanted to know how something *made me feel*. She was very good at expressing her feelings. I was brought up in a home with my mom and dad and three brothers. We didn't really need to say a whole lot. I don't remember talking about how we felt. So when Elaine wanted to know how a certain situation "made me feel," I could not express it because I honestly didn't know. Becoming familiar with my emotional world was a challenge. It started when a friend explained: "Tim, there are only four general categories of feelings - Mad, Sad, Glad, and Scared. When Elaine asks how you feel, see which of the four feelings you're experiencing." This helped me tremendously.

Elaine's ability to "out-talk" me was very intimidating. At first, I tried to avoid it as much as possible. However, it became very clear that if we were going to resolve our conflicts appropriately, I would need to learn to communicate better.

Understanding two basic concepts helped me. 1) The purpose of communication is to *connect*, not just exchange information. 2) The goal of every conversation is to understand and be understood. Knowing I had only two objectives made things rather simple for me (not easy, but simple).

Learning to skillfully communicate has been a life-long process which continues today. I frequently remind myself to listen in order to understand. Old habits die hard, so I continue to work on sending a clear message when I need to be understood.

Mutual Respect

Love each other with genuine affection, and take delight in honoring each other (Romans 12:10 - NLT).

Mutual respect is the concept of *giving honor to whom honor is due* (Rom. 13:7). It is living according to the Golden Rule (Luke 6:31). *Do to others as you would have them do to you* (Lk. 6:31 NIV). Miriam-Webster defines respect as: *a feeling or understanding that someone or something is important, serious, etc., and should be treated in an appropriate way.*

During an interview with a couple who celebrated their 50th wedding anniversary, I asked them to list three reasons their relationship had lasted so long and what advice they would give to young couples. They listed mutual respect, showing grace, and forgiveness. The concept of respect is not as simple as I would like. What evokes respect for another person? Respect seems to come easier for a person who shares our values. It is easy to respect someone for their honorable acts. But how does a person respect someone they genuinely do not respect? Certainly, a person's positive performance, choices, and attitudes can evoke respect, even if you disagree strongly with that person's opinions. Other qualities, like a strong commitment to beliefs and values, give reason for respect. But how do you respect a husband or wife whose performance and choices create problems for you?

It can certainly be said that respect is a choice one makes. The Echrichs, in their book *Love and Respect*, suggest that, just as unconditional love is a choice, so is unconditional respect. This is a great point. However, upon what basis does a spouse respect the person who has failed repeatedly and continues to offend? What can this person focus on in order to show respect?

At its basic level, respect is based upon human dignity. Although it is much easier to respect a person whose qualities naturally evoke respect, the failure of a spouse and the disappointment that follows are not reasons to withhold respect. We must be careful to guard our hearts against falling into this subtle trap (Rom. 12:3; 12:10; 14:4; Phil. 2:3).

Being courteous, showing kindness, and being thoughtful and considerate are all intentional ways to build up your mate and add resources to your marriage. It is easy to take a person for granted and minimize or ignore their opinions. It is easy to allow differences to divide you. When you make the effort to appreciate your wife's differences and accept her unconditionally, you help create an environment for growth. When you allow your spouse to be who she is, without trying to change her, you allow positive income to flow into your marriage. When you view your spouse as a gift from God (rather than an opponent or an enemy), you will develop an attitude that pleases the Lord and causes you to experience God's blessing in your relationship and family.

As you become intentional about being kind, generous, and courteous (Rom. 12:10) toward your mate; when you look, not only to your own interests and needs, but to those of your wife (Phil. 2:3), your efforts, out of a desire to please the Lord, will bring income into your marriage. These Income Sources provide a reservoir of resources that help you through the dry times—those desert seasons that every marriage encounters.

Realistic Expectations

What did you expect from marriage? From your spouse? Every person goes into marriage with expectations, even if they have not been identified. Some expectations show up when your spouse disappoints you. Unspoken expectations can be a drain on marital resources. A new wife expects her husband to fix things around the house like her dad did. She never actually communicated this to him. When he says, "I don't know how to fix a leaky faucet," she doesn't know how to respond. She is disappointed. This may be a light disappointment, but it is an example of how unspoken or unrealistic expectations unfairly place your spouse in a no-win situation.

Understanding the limitations of your spouse and your marriage is critical. Good communication is necessary to sort out what can be expected and what cannot. What do you expect from your spouse? Have you communicated this to her? It is a rare person who doesn't fall prey to this trap. It is a rare couple who has taken the time to talk about their expectations. But for those who do, their potential for unnecessary conflict is greatly reduced.

Being realistic about growth and change is also essential. Unfortunately, growth and change come slowly for us all. You are going to have disagreements and conflicts. Being realistic about the challenges will prove to be very positive. Your spouse is human just like you. She will disappoint you. She may hurt you. Having realistic expectations is an Income Source because it helps you to be more understanding and patient. It helps you practice walking in forgiveness. It helps you keep short accounts, be more gracious, and show mercy toward your mate.

Remember, you are married to a sinner (as is the case for your spouse). You must give each other room to grow. Your marriage is a marathon, not a sprint. The establishing phase takes time and requires perseverance and patience. Having realistic expectations can provide many benefits for your relationship—benefits that will enable you to have a lasting and enduring marriage.

Practicing Forgiveness

Forgiveness is not something that comes naturally. To forgive means to *release from a debt*. It is a choice we make to release a person from a debt owed while extending the same mercy we received from God. Forgiveness not only releases a person from a debt owed, but it has a cleansing effect (1 John 1:9). It changes the relationship. God's forgiveness toward sinners creates a new identity in those who trust Jesus and the Gospel. Forgiveness changes who we are. What was broken is mended. What was dead is now alive.

Like vertical forgiveness, forgiveness between two individuals is designed to bring healing. The truth is, holding on to offenses is destructive. It may feel right and even appropriate. But it eats away at love in every possible way. Perhaps that is why God instructs us to forgive even our enemies. It is a gift we share with someone who, like us, does not deserve it. It says we are both in need of the same help.

There are times when we resist the idea of forgiveness in an attempt to protect and defend ourselves. In marriage (as in all close relationships), we cannot avoid offending one another. Choosing to walk in forgiveness toward your spouse will help you show love rather than becoming defensive. Most of us desire mercy for ourselves when we behave badly and make poor choices. After all, God is merciful. Yet, when someone offends us, we lean toward the justice side of God's character and demand that the offending party pay for what he or she did.

The Apostle Peter asked Jesus the question that has crossed every offended person's mind: *how often shall my brother sin against me, and I forgive him? Up to seven times?" Jesus said to him, "I do not say to you, up to seven times, but up to seventy times seven* (Matthew 18:21-22). Of course, Jesus is not suggesting keeping a ledger of 490 offenses, then bringing judgment down on the offending party. He is suggesting that keeping records of offenses is unnecessary. He is showing us a path of forgiveness, a way of living life.

Walking in forgiveness implies an understanding that we will inevitably be offended by others (Matt. 18:7). Therefore, we must choose in advance how we will respond. How you react to your spouse's offenses will determine your future together. Walking in forgiveness creates an environment for growth and strength.

Friends and Fun

A friend loves at all times (Proverbs 17:17).

Being good friends and having fun together is what most couples build their relationships on in their early days. Couples can remember spending time together, having long conversations, and simply enjoying being in each other's company. The pressures and demands of life have a way of choking out, not only the fun in a marriage, but its very life.

In marriage, friendship is vital. Friends look out for each other. Friends care what happens to the other. Friends invest in each other's best interests. In his book, *The Seven Principles for Making Marriage Work,* Dr. John Gottman confidently affirms that "happy marriages are based on a deep friendship. In the strongest marriages, husband and wife share a deep sense of meaning. They don't just 'get along'-- they also support each other's hopes and aspirations and build a sense of purpose into their lives together."

One of the worst things that can happen to any relationship is for one person to view the other as an enemy. What you believe about your wife determines how you interact with her. If you believe she is safe, you may risk being vulnerable. If you believe she is against you, you will protect yourself.

A friend loves at all times and being a good friend requires intentionality. (Prov. 17:17; 18:24). Jesus said, *give and it shall be given to you* (Lk 6:38). It is the Biblical principle of sowing and reaping (Gal. 6:7-8). You plant (invest) into your spouse the things that you desire. As you invest in each other, your marriage becomes stronger and you will have a lot more fun together. If you have neglected your friendship, if you have allowed busyness and problems to steal your time together, you can make changes that will steer you back in the right direction, even if those changes are small baby steps. What does your wife enjoy? What did you do together in the past that you both enjoyed? Begin seeing these little choices and activities as Income Sources that you cannot afford to neglect.

One of the ways to facilitate friendship and fun is to have regular dates.

Regular Dates

Elaine and I started having regular dates when our girls were very young. Small children, work, financial challenges and life itself created many demands on our marriage. We knew we should be taking time for each other, but we didn't have any. It was already claimed by other things. We were running on empty and feeling the strain on our relationship. We had to make a change. No one was coming to rescue us. We had to assume responsibility. It was our relationship and we needed to take action.

Added to our already overly demanding schedule was my personal struggle with depression. It was a dark time in my life and in our marriage and we really didn't know what to do to combat it. It was during this dark season that we decided that one night every week would be for just the two of us. We asked friends, who were in the same situation as we were, if we could trade watching each other's children for date night. They would watch ours while we took the night off and we would do the same for them. It was only for a couple hours, but it was so nice and it worked great!

For us, dating was a commitment that we honored. Even when we were experiencing conflict and really didn't feel like being around each other, we went on our date anyway! And usually, we were able to clear the air and end up enjoying our time together.

Today, even though our children are adults, Elaine and I still have regular dates. It continues to be an Income Source for us.

Time Away Together

Getting away for a night or two, breaking away from your routine, and being in a new environment can bring you a fresh perspective. Most couples will attest to the fact that getting away alone without any of the normal distractions of life can create an environment for connection and intimacy. Whether it is an afternoon at the park or a week at your favorite resort, these getaways are necessary for building into your marriage.

Romantic and Physical Enjoyment

The bride in the Song of Solomon says, *When I found the one I loved, I held him and would not let him go...do not stir up or awaken love until it pleases* (Song 3:4-5). There's a place in marriage for playfulness, just having fun together. There is also a place for being alone, naked and unashamed (Gen. 2:25). Enjoying one another and keeping that special part of your relationship pure is one of the best kept secrets of marriage. Hollywood propagates the notion that marriage is boring and that real excitement is found in relationships with no commitments. Yet married couples experience an excitement and fulfillment that can only be found in the confines of marital commitment. God created us with the capacity for sexual desire and arousal. We are sexual beings and He wants us to enjoy one another.

There is an interesting story in the book of Genesis that gives us a window into Isaac and Rebekah's relationship. We are told that Isaac, following his father's example (Gen. 12), lied to King Abimalech about Rebekah, saying she was not his wife but his sister. Listen to this very insightful comment in Genesis 26:8: *Abimelech king of the Philistines looked through a window, and saw, and there was Isaac, showing endearment to Rebekah his wife* (NKJV). The word translated *endearment* means to be playful. In other references, the word is translated *to laugh* (Gen. 18:12). Isaac and Rebekah were playfully enjoying one another and the King instantly knew they were not brother and sister.

A husband or wife may struggle being sexually intimate because of past experiences or trauma. There are resources available that can help you address these difficulties. [6] Other spouses have a difficult time seeing their sexual relationship in reference to God. Your romantic and sexual relationship should be approached with the same attitude as worship. The Lord sees all and knows all and desires the best for you.

To share intimate time in a safe environment is a great Income Source in marriage. It is no wonder that the enemy does whatever he can to separate us from each other.

Spiritual Intimacy

As I stated earlier in the prayer category, spiritual intimacy is one of the areas of marriage that is sometimes difficult even for Christian couples. The Apostle Peter writes, *Husbands likewise dwell with them, your wives, with understanding, giving honor to the wife as to the weaker vessel, and as being heirs together of the grace of life that your prayers may not be hindered.* (1 Pet. 3:7). This passage emphasizes the benefits of developing spiritual intimacy as couples: *the grace of life.* It also cautions us not to ignore the importance of understanding and the vital role spiritual unity plays in experiencing God's blessings. You and your spouse are *heirs together.* You are a team. Covenant partners.

Spiritual Intimacy is not limited to praying together. Reading and studying God's Word can be a great Income Source. Spiritual discussions about how God's Word can be practically applied to life can bring deeper intimacy. Singing together; worshipping together; serving together--these activities provide vehicles for Income to flow into your marriage.

Attend Church Together. You have probably heard that going to church makes you a Christian as much as going to McDonalds makes you a hamburger. That's probably true. However, going to church regularly may help your marriage.

Shaunti Feldhahn, in her book *The Good News About Marriage* cites several studies showing positive contributors to a lasting marriage. She points to 2002 reports by the CDC/NSFG showing that those who said faith was "very important" to them had a 28 percent lower divorce rate. Another report found that "evangelicals who attended church weekly decreased their rate of divorce by 22 percent over those evangelicals who never attended.

The *Family Needs Survey,* conducted by FamilyLife, found that those who prayed or read the Bible together in any kind of regular way, even just a few times a month, cut their marital danger signals in half. The point is that attending church together is something that is likely to enhance your marriage, and it is something you can start doing soon.

Teamwork

Fostering teamwork as a couple is not only important, it is also a great source of Income for your marriage. Working together to accomplish your dreams, parenting as a team, and planning and working to provide for your financial future are just a few items that require teamwork in marriage.

Marriage provides an opportunity to live for something greater than yourself. You cannot be self-centered and successful in your marriage. Marriage requires joining your life with another and pooling your resources and energy for a greater cause than personal happiness. Every failed marriage has self-interests to blame for its demise. Couples who learn to function as a team have greater rewards to celebrate.

In sports, it doesn't matter how talented and skilled individual players are. If they do not learn how to function as a team, they will not be successful. The same is true for marriage. Each spouse brings specific strengths and weaknesses to the team. Understanding each other's strengths and weaknesses plays a huge role in the success of your team.

Marriage and family life is about serving, not being served. When you willingly sacrifice for another, God honors your sacrifice. The Preacher wrote, *two are better than one, because they have a good reward for their labor* (Eccl. 4:9). God put you and your spouse together for more reasons than you might know or understand. As team players, you learn to *prefer one another* (Phil. 2:3). When you choose to function as a team, something very positive happens to your marriage. Your relationship becomes stronger.

Identify Specific Income Sources

The above list of Income Sources is common. In most cases, these Income Sources will provide your marriage with necessary Income.

If you are having difficulty thinking of potential Income Sources, here are a few suggestions:

- Think about things you used to do together for fun.
- Look through your local community calendar of events to see if there is something you may be interested in.
- Look around you. Are there couples in your life who do things together? Ask them for ideas.

Part-time Income

Ideally, you want to have a constant stream of marital income flowing into your relationship. However, there may be times when your current income is not adequate for unexpected needs that emerge. An unexpected illness, a house fire, or any event that places demands on your marriage can quickly deplete your marital resources. In these times, you will need to make sacrifices to increase your marital income. You may want to attend a marriage seminar or workshop. You may join a small group study on marriage or get training in a particular area of marriage.

You may need to seek Biblical marriage counseling. If you need assistance, you may contact our office.[7] There are times when a couple may find themselves in circumstances where they cannot get out of their relational ruts without the help of an objective party. They may benefit from intentional time set aside to deal with issues they have not addressed properly. Proverbs 11:14 says, *where no counsel is, the people fall, but in the multitude of counselors, there is safety.*

Income is not Free

Every Income Source requires some form of expenses and sacrifice. Like starting a new business or job, you will need to purchase items and carve out time to make your new venture a success. You have to make an investment. And your investment is intended to produce needed income.

Work on Your Marriage Budget (Individual Worksheet)

Turn to your individual *Marriage Budget* worksheet (Appendix A).

Now you have the opportunity to begin the process of assessing your Income Sources from a personal perspective.

Current Income Sources

Think of activities that may assist you in building your relationship. At this point, only think about things from your perspective. Do not consult your spouse (you will have the opportunity to do this later). In the left Income Source column, list the things *you* consider Current Income Sources for your marriage. You may scan the last six to twelve months to list what things have added to your relationship.

Additional Income Sources

After you have listed what you think are Current Income Sources, think about things that could potentially become Income Sources (right column). These items will be helpful when you and your spouse compare your budgets. These items may be things you personally would enjoy or things your spouse might enjoy. This is also where you would list things you have enjoyed in the past that you can reintroduce to your relationship.

NOTE: An Income Source can be something one spouse does for the other. For example, I enjoy fishing. Elaine does not. But she loves to read. So, to invest in our marriage, she will sit in the boat with me and read while I fish my heart out. She sacrifices for something I enjoy, and it adds to our relationship (even though I don't usually catch many fish!).

Once you have completed the Individual Marriage Budget, you and your spouse can compare each budget and work together to come up with your Marriage Budget. I will cover this in Chapter 7. You can find a summary of Common Income Sources in Appendix C.

Individual Budget

1. Income Sources that you currently have (left column). Do not be concerned with whether your spouse thinks these are Income Sources. List what you think.
2. Next, list any Additional (new) activities that you think may be good Income Sources (Right Column). This can be something you can do alone (like bringing your spouse coffee in bed) or something you can do as a couple.

Join the conversation on Facebook. Share how this chapter has been beneficial to you.
https://www.facebook.com/managingyourmarriage

Chapter 3

Necessary Expenses

A Necessary Expense is something that costs you, but is necessary for your relationship.

In a financial budget, necessary household expenses would include things like electricity, food, clothing, etc. These things are necessary to run a household and keep your family sustained. You cannot really function without them (at least in the common American home). Because these are necessary expenses, they require resources. You may wish you did not need some things, but you do. The same is true for your marriage.

In some cases, an item you list as an Income Source on your *Marriage Budget Worksheet* will also be listed under Necessary Expenses. For example, Elaine and I take time for conversation most mornings (coffee time). This is an Income Source. However, in order for us to maintain this time and carve it out of our schedule, it requires effort. It costs us time that we could both use for other things. Good communication requires work! Therefore, communication, although it is an Income Source, is also a Necessary Expense.

To get a better idea of Marital Expenses, read the examples below. You will have the opportunity to complete your marriage budget later.

Common Necessary Expenses
Learn Good Communication Skills

Communication is something we continually work on. Learning good communication skills is necessary and requires being honest about our tendencies.

As I mentioned earlier, Elaine and I came into our marriage with different communication styles. Elaine was matter-of-fact in the way she communicated and paid close attention to details. I was more passive and wanted to smooth things over. As you might imagine, getting to a place where we could effectively communicate required lots of work. I have learned so much about communication from Elaine. But in the early days of our marriage, I was not as appreciative of her communication style. Along with my tendency toward passivity, there was a strong desire to avoid conflict. Our different communication styles created huge obstacles in our marriage. Because we misunderstood each other, we could not communicate effectively and therefore did not resolve conflict very well.

Learning better communication skills may require reading a book (or several) on the topic. Because of the powerful component of habits, you will need to allow others to help you when you habitually do things that are counterproductive, like interrupting, rolling your eyes, not seeking to understand, etc.

Communication is an essential skill for a healthy marriage. The inability or unwillingness to communicate is an expense you cannot afford. Do what you must to learn good communication skills. God's Word is the best resource for developing these skills.

Financial Issues

Managing, organizing, and monitoring finances in your home is a Necessary Expense. It requires time and communication from a couple. It takes effort and it requires commitment. The ongoing demands of good stewardship resources. To neglect our financial responsibilities is to invite trouble into our marriage.

Couples who fight about finances usually engage in blame shifting, accusations, and angry outbursts. Being committed to effectively communicate about financial matters can help you avoid unnecessary conflict in your relationship. Communicating respectfully about spending, saving, and unexpected expenses will help provide an environment for unity and teamwork.

Because money problems are a major cause for marriage problems, it is worth the time and effort necessary to learn better management skills. When a couple neglects doing the hard work required to manage their finances, this easily moves from the Expense category to the debt category (which we will look at later). For some couples, the area of finances has become a huge burden and may need to be listed in the Marital Debt Column (next chapter).

Children (Parenting)

Another common Expense for couples is children and their varied needs and demands. Experienced parents know how difficult training children can be. If you have multiple children, you know that their needs are not necessarily the same. For example, the way you communicate with one child may not work as well with another.

Parental unity may be the most powerful asset you have as parents. Conversely, disunity can create tremendous chaos in a family. Whether it's your style of communication, methods of discipline, priorities of scheduling activities, or a host of other decisions impacting your family, parental unity needs to be pursued.

One of our many lessons as parents was due to the fact that our girls were so close in age. Thus, it was convenient for us to do things together. We sort of clumped them into a group. The challenge became helping them develop as individuals rather than group members. One of the things we did that helped was to allow each one to stay up 30 minutes longer than her sisters, one night each week. This was "her time" to spend with mom and dad. She decided what we did for 30 minutes. We could talk, play a game, sing, or read; it was up to her.

Another invaluable addition to our repertoire of parenting practices was taking a weekend away every January to pray for our children and talk about what their unique needs and challenges were. This was more of a work weekend for us than It was for pleasure. But it was work the effort. Because we wanted to be the best parents we could and because we knew that the Lord had a plan for our family, we did what was necessary to the best of our ability.

Elaine and I have said to one another many times through the years, "We would do it all over again." The Lord taught us so many valuable lessons through this Necessary Expense; lessons we would not have learned any other way.

Complications during pregnancy, adjusting to a new baby, and adjusting to the adolescent and teenage years are examples of demands that are necessary and require marital income.

Praying Together

Even though prayer is an Income Source, it requires effort and thus it is also a Necessary Expense. Many couples think praying together is a good idea but find it very challenging. In some cases, a husband and wife are fine praying as individuals, yet when it comes to praying as a couple, they struggle.

Praying together is a benefit worth the effort. I suggest to couples who want to begin praying together to commit to a couple of minutes. The objective is not to pray for long periods of time but to take small steps toward becoming comfortable praying together. You may begin by thanking the Lord for His blessings. Read the Lord's Prayer aloud (Matt. 6). Some couples hold hands. They find that touching each other while in prayer helps them to bond.

The more you become accustomed to praying aloud in each other's presence, the more connected you will begin to feel. This effort of connecting spiritually becomes an Income Source for your relationship.

Regular Dates

Making time to plan regular dates is a Necessary Expense in order to gain Marital Income. Whether it is an evening out for dinner and fun or week-long vacation, planning requires work. The more detailed the date, the more planning it requires. Many couples find simple and inexpensive ways to have their dates. Some take walks together. Others go to the lake or the beach. If you are not a natural "dater" you will need to do some research. I have listed a few resources for date ideas. See footnote.[8]

Resolving Conflict

Learning to resolve conflicts Biblically is probably one the best kept secrets of a happy marriage. When it comes to understanding and resolving conflict, defining terms can be helpful

Three Levels of Conflict

Three words have helped couples better understand the concept and context of conflict.

The first word is *disagreement*. Every couple has disagreements. We are different, and those differences show up in many areas of life. It can be as simple as the color of a wall or our favorite food. Disagreements are not negative. In fact, it is through disagreements that we learn about our mate and grow in understanding. There is absolutely nothing wrong with a couple having a disagreement. It not considered a "fight" when you disagree.

The second word is *argument*. When a couple says, "We had an argument." What does that mean to you? Do you think they were in a knock-down-drag-out fight? People mean different things when they use the word argue. Technically, an argument is not a fight.

An *argument* is best understood in a courtroom setting. One attorney presents his or her side of the argument. Then the other attorney does the same. To an observer, it may appear that these attorneys are enemies. However, it is possible that they are very good friends and may even share their thoughts over dinner at the end of the day. Each presents his argument with passion in an attempt to persuade the jury to see things from their perspective. Both are using the same evidence to argue for their client. They are presenting their *argument*...the way they see it.

Couples who are on a growth track usually argue about the things they disagree about. A good respectful argument can be a very productive thing. Through it, you may realize you have blind spots. You may also grow in your understanding of the subject and the person with whom you are arguing.

The third word is *fight*. Conflict is defined as *a fight, battle, or struggle, especially a prolonged struggle; strife* (www.Dictionary.com) A conflict is war! And usually, this kind of couple interaction is always a lose-lose combination. When a couple enters this volatile territory, something or someone will inevitably be damaged. I do not believe it is ever necessary for a couple to go to this level in their relationship. With good communication and conflict resolution skills, a couple should be able to resolve things in a mature and respectful manner.

If you have bad communication habits which propel you into destructive fights, you have work to do. If you learn how to argue and use Biblical principles, you should never have to get to a place where you are in an outright fight.

Unexpected Challenges

Unexpected challenges in a marriage come in many different forms. One couple struggles with infertility while another grapples with the loss of a job. One couple struggles due to past abuse, while another deals with the horrible effects of an accident.

One of my "unexpected challenges" was due to me not being familiar with the world of women and being unaware of "that time of the month." Remember, I didn't have a sister growing up. For me, this required a major adjustment. During these times, Elaine would relate to me differently than normal. It would catch me off-guard every month.

The challenge intensified as our four teenage daughters joined my wife. There was not a week in our home that did not present challenges for me to learn patience. Eventually, I became more educated about the world of women and started marking my calendar so that I would be prepared.

God uses unexpected challenges to grow us! They are Necessary Expenses that cannot be avoided. They require work! These challenges reveal things about us that we may have never known, both good and bad. By viewing unexpected challenges as necessary opportunities for growth, you can minimize the amount of emotional resources required and thus preserve these valuable resources for other Necessary Expenses.

Emotional Struggles

Whether it is depression, stress, or anything of that nature, emotional struggles demand effort from both the sufferer and the spouse. Emotional struggles can come from anything: an illness, infertility, the loss of a loved one through death, the loss of a job, or some other loss. If you are the one struggling with emotional issues, you bear a heavy burden and will have to learn to navigate through your dark season with God's help and perhaps the assistance of others. The good news is that you will not have to live this way forever! There is hope! If, however, you are the spouse of one who is struggling emotionally, you will have to work at becoming more understanding and supportive. You will be required to make personal sacrifices. The Preacher writes: *Two are better than one...for if they fall, one will lift up his companion. But woe to him who is alone when he falls, for he has no one to help him up* (Eccl. 4:9).

As a child, I endured some traumatic experiences. In the beginning months of dealing with the impact of this trauma, I experienced seasons of deep depression. Neither Elaine nor I understood exactly what was happening. In one of my darkest times, I remember Elaine saying to me, "I don't understand what we are going through or why, but I am here with you and we will get through this together." She was correct, and I am forever grateful for her and her commitment to me.

If your spouse experiences dark emotional seasons, loving him or her will require patient support, care, compassion, and probably some self-sacrifice. You may not fully understand. You may not know how to fix it. But you will sacrifice to get your spouse through their dark season. In God's Sovereign plan, this difficult challenge was presented to you. And by His grace and through His strength, you will get through this and you will both be the better for it!

Decision Making

Making decisions in general can be a Necessary Expense. This is an area where you and your spouse's differences may present problems. Some people make decisions off the cuff, without much forethought. Others are planners and need to ponder their decisions carefully. Because the decisions you make will affect your spouse, decision making needs to include good communication skills, patience, and consideration of each other.

I remember the time I decided we needed a new car. I hated the big bulky Pontiac we owned, even though it was in good running condition and paid for! I was determined to buy a new car. Elaine did not agree. She said, "I do not agree with this decision." Today, that comment would send up a bright flag of caution, but it did not detour me at all then. I bought a new car; a brand new sporty looking Datsun (today it's Nissan) with a five speed transmission. I was very excited! Elaine did not share in that excitement. Everything about that car was great except for the fact that it did not have air conditioning. Of course, when I bought the car, it was the middle of winter. When the hot and humid summer days of South Louisiana approached, I started feeling the error of my way. Elaine was very gracious in not saying "I told you so," and the Lord was gracious in providing a buyer. But the lesson I learned has stayed with me; Elaine and I need to be in agreement on major decisions. Her input is valuable and beneficial. That policy has been part of our marriage since that day. My self-will created Unnecessary Expenses for our marriage, which we will cover next.

Aging Parents

A Necessary Expense that younger couples rarely think about is aging parents. My dad died when he was 87. My mom followed him ten months later, at age 86. Both were under Hospice care and due to the closeness of their illnesses and deaths, many decisions had to be made that required emotional resources. Elaine's dad died a couple years later, after dealing with several physical problems. During the days leading up to their deaths, Elaine and I made several trips that required many days away from work and from our ongoing responsibilities. Opportunities to honor parents may not come at the most convenient time, but the responsibility to help care for our parents is a Necessary Expense. Because you care, you sacrifice and serve.

There are many Necessary Expenses in marriage that I did not list. Your marriage and family is unique with unique challenges and needs. You may have Marriage Expenses that your friends do not have. You may be tempted to complain and view others' circumstances as better than yours. Be careful! Instead of looking for a way out, look for God's hand in your specific situation and seek to honor Him in and through it.

Work on Your Marriage Budget (Individual Worksheet)

Turn to your individual *Marriage Budget* worksheet (Appendix A) and list the current Necessary Expenses you are aware of in the left column of the Individual *Marriage Budget Worksheet*. After listing your Current Unnecessary Expenses, list a few items that you may need to *add* (in the right column) in order to get more Income into your marriage. You can find a summary of Common Income Sources in Appendix D.

Once you have completed the Individual Budget, you and your spouse can compare each budget and work together to come up with your Marriage Budget. I will cover this in Chapter 7.

Join the conversation on Facebook. Share how this chapter has been beneficial to you.
https://www.facebook.com/managingyourmarriage

Chapter 4
Unnecessary Expenses

Catch all the foxes, those little foxes, before they ruin the vineyard of love, for the grapevines are blossoming! (Song 2:15)

An unnecessary expense is something your marriage cannot afford.

Unnecessary Expenses are liabilities that take away needed resources from your relationship. To use a financial budget example again, if you are spending forty dollars a week for ice cream, and you do not have enough money to buy your child's school supplies, something is wrong! Your ice cream habit is an Unnecessary Expense that you cannot afford. If you have ten subscriptions to the same magazine genre, and you cannot afford it, this is an Unnecessary Expense. You may desire a more expensive car than you can afford, but you must choose to live within your means. In the same way, marriage management requires good stewardship of the resources we have.

Common Unnecessary Expenses
Busy Schedules (Overly committed)

Whether it is work, school, extracurricular activities, or simply keeping up with necessary home maintenance, most American families are stretched to their limit. Busyness is one of the subtle killers of marriage and quality family time. If you have a difficult time saying "no" to opportunities that come your way, you will find yourself among those who live very frantic lives. It becomes a case of "The tail is wagging the dog." Out of control lives make for stressed-filled and frustrated relationships.

God gave the Children of Israel a command to rest. It was so important that it made the top ten list, coming in at number four. *Remember the Sabbath day, to keep it holy* (Ex. 20:8). The word Sabbath comes from the Hebrew word *shabbath* meaning "intermission." I have often thought that the Lord's reason for making *rest* mandatory was because the Children of Israel would not have thought of resting as being that important. For most of us, the idea of rest seems like a waste of good productive time. However, those who have experienced burnout will acknowledge that if they had to do things over, they would take more time to rest.

As important as church and community life is, you may need to assess your level of involvement. Many well-meaning couples commit far too much time helping out at church, in their community, or with friends. You may have good intentions. You may see these requests as opportunities to serve. If your commitments are such that you are neglecting your spouse and children, you would be wise to make a few changes.

Perhaps you and your spouse need to discuss priorities and make a few hard choices concerning your schedules. You will find that as you value God's Word on this issue, you will be more at peace and likely more productive. Good stewardship requires taking control of our schedules and deciding on what is reasonable, healthy, and affordable. You must work at removing the things that are draining and depleting your relationship resources.

Unnecessary Arguments

Not every disagreement needs to be argued. Elaine and I can simply agree to disagree on matters that involve preferences. I like Chinese food and she prefers anything else. That's totally okay. One of my old habits (and one that still shows up at times) is choosing to be defensive when Elaine brings up an area that we disagree about. When she would bring up a topic, even though bringing it up was good and right, I would feel the need to defend myself. I would explain how I had improved a little! Of course, we were not discussing how much or how little I had improved. Elaine was communicating to me something that was important to her. My choice to defend myself propelled us into unnecessary arguments that could have easily been avoided.

I have spoken with many couples who experience this in the car. The husband is driving. As he approaches a stop sign, his wife says, "Stop sign." He says, "I see it!" As he approaches a traffic signal, she says, "Red light." He begins to feel irritated. Before he can find words to express his irritation, she says, "Green light."

I smile as I write these words, because this scenario has taken place in our car many times. I realize now that Elaine is not trying to tell me how to drive. She says these things for herself. Even though I don't fully understand why she needs to articulate these things, it helps me to not takes her words personally and that makes for a much more pleasant trip.

We must choose our battles. Unnecessary Expenses deplete our emotional resources.

Gottman's Four Horsemen

Researcher, Dr. John Gottman, has spent over 30 years working with couples. His research has identified four destructive components at work in marriages that fail. He calls these, "The Four Horsemen of the Apocalypse." Dr. Gottman suggests that these components show up in every marriage, but when they take up permanent residence, they create huge problems. I have outlined the Four here:

1. *Criticism*: Unlike issuing a complaint, Criticism is an attack on your partner's character. It implies that the person has something wrong with them. These statements usually begin with "you always...," "you never...," etc. Gottman suggests that the same negative impact can come in the form of questions: "Why don't you care about me?" Why are you so inconsiderate?"

2. *Contempt*: Contempt is a first cousin to *disdain, scorn, strong feelings of disapproval.* Contempt can come in verbal or non-verbal messages. These messages are latent with sarcasm, cynicism and insults. Name-calling, rolling the eyes, and disgust, coupled with a posture that implies one partner is below the other and is looked down upon, can be especially destructive. According to Gottman, it is the most poisonous of the Four Horsemen.

3. *Defensiveness*: Gottman suggests that these Four Horsemen come in sequential order. It makes sense that if a spouse perceives he is being attacked (contempt), defending himself is reasonable.

The defender assumes the posture of a victim. "Why are you attacking me?" He or she may deflect the criticism by issuing a corresponding attack or accusation. "Well, what about you? Do you think you do everything right?"

The defender tends to avoid taking responsibility and offers excuses, which only angers the spouse who issued the criticism. Deflecting, avoiding, whining, and creating a diversion by changing the subject are all ways of defending oneself.

4. *Stonewalling*: Gottman explains that Stonewalling occurs when a spouse stops listening and withdraws from the relationship. They disengage. Stonewalling can come in the form of avoiding conflict, refusing to answer a question, looking away, or habitually escaping through hobbies, television, shopping with friends, etc.

Gottman's findings revealed that men (85%) are more likely to stonewall than women. The person stonewalling may agree with an accusation ("I know I do that.") in an attempt to brush a spouse off and avoid genuine engagement. He or she may think it is honorable to not argue. The truth is, stonewalling sends a negative message of rejection to a spouse.

Apathy

The opposite of love is not hate, it's indifference. Elie Weisel

Apathy is defined as a *lack of feeling or emotion*. Simply stated, apathy or indifference reveals an attitude of not caring. Apathy can set in when a spouse feels he has exasperated all attempts at solving a problem.

John and Mary came to an impasse in their relationship. John felt he had tried everything possible to please Mary, yet she continued to complain that he wasn't loving her. Mary felt that John's actions were rote; he was simply checking items off his list of things to do. She wanted him to *want* to do things for her. John, became frustrated when it seemed every effort was met with a criticism of how he could have done it better. John became exasperated and gave up. He concluded: *I cannot please her!* So he quit trying.

In the same way voters become apathetic with the political process and feel their votes will do no good, apathy in marriage draws a similar conclusion: "What's the use? Why Try? Why have this conversation again? We never solve the problem!"

When people care about something deeply, they engage others. Even intense arguments retain the necessary component of asserting what you believe is important. When a person gives up on their marriage, they stop fighting for it. They stop loving. They stop caring.

Your marriage cannot afford apathy. It is understandable that you might become very discouraged. But to embrace apathy implies that you believe all hope is gone and that even God cannot help.

The truth is, God wants you to trust Him, to lean upon Him, and to look to Him for guidance and wisdom. You cannot afford to give up on your marriage. You must stay engaged in the process of personal growth and pursuing marital unity. Love requires it! Love *bears all things, believes all things, hopes all things, endures all things. Love never fails!* (1 Cor. 13:7-8)

You may not know what the solution is at this time, but you cannot afford to lose hope, give up, and become apathetic.

Selfishness

The essence of our fallen condition and the most common cause for marriage problems is selfishness. Selfishness can be overt and obvious, or it can show up in very subtle ways.

The best marriages are those where a husband and wife try to out serve each other. A story I have shared many times, (although I don't remember where I originally heard it) can help us with perspective. A man dreamed he went to hell. He found himself in a long rectangular room with long rows of tables and chairs positioned as they would be in a banquet hall. People were seated across from one another. The strange thing was, no one was able to bend their elbows. The environment was unpleasant. People were throwing their food into the air, trying to catch it with their opened mouths. It was a mess and everyone seemed frustrated. In the next scene of his dream, the man was in heaven. The seating arrangements were the same and no one could bend their elbows. However, the atmosphere was pleasant and cheerful. Instead of people trying to feed themselves, they had learned to feed one another across the table. By meeting the other's needs, their needs were met.

Selfishness can produce an array of offensive behaviors in marriage. Yet because selfishness is so ingrained in us, it is not always easy to detect. We are not always aware when our attitudes and choices are motivated to please self.

Of course, selfishness is not a quality of love. Love *does not seek its own* (1 Cor. 13:5). It seeks what is best for the other person. Love is willing to sacrifice and give for another; selfishness is stingy and demands its way. We may never love perfectly. Even on our best and most generous days, selfishness can show up, asking how this giving might benefit me.

People generally fall into one of two broad categories. We tend to be givers or takers. No one wants to see himself as a taker; it takes a courageous person to admit it when he or she realizes taking from others is his or her normal posture. However, without recognizing and admitting our selfishness, we can never overcome it. At the end of the day, because of our broken condition, we are all takers. We all want our desires met.

Selfishness blinds us from seeing others' needs. If you are in the habit of taking, you have developed the habit through consistent practice (and you have probably become very good at it). Learning to consider your spouse may be a difficult challenge, but it is a challenge you must step into with God's help. Learning to love is our greatest objective and our greatest need (Matt. 22:37-40).

Selfish Demands

When desires are viewed as needs, they can easily become demands.

The Apostle Paul urges the Philippians: *Let each of you look out not only for his own interests, but also for the interests of others* (Phil. 2:4).

Every spouse has God-given desires. A husband desires respect and admiration from his wife. A wife desires to be loved, cared for, and protected by her husband. These desires are natural, good, and appropriate in marriage.

A common mistake we make is thinking that a desire is a need. When we perceive desires as needs, we create a fundamental shift in our thinking. And we are one step away from selfish demands. For example, if a husband views his sexual desires as sexual needs, he will begin to feel deprived of something that he feels is necessary to his survival. He may even justify looking outside his marriage relationship in an attempt to meet his perceived *need*. His mistaken belief can easily cause him to progress from sharing his desires with his wife, to demanding she "meet his need."

A wife may deeply desire for her husband to be conversational and to share his heart with her. This is a legitimate desire and there is nothing wrong with it. However, if she perceives her desire as a need, she may complain that he doesn't love her. She can easily be entrapped by the misbelief that deep, heart-felt conversation is something she needs (i.e. must have) and that her husband should meet her need. Her desires turn into a demand.

When you demand that your spouse satisfy your desires, you are attempting to force your mate to do something he or she may not be ready and able to do. The focus is no longer on your spouse or your marriage, it is now only about you. Forcing your spouse to meet your perceived needs may seem like a solution temporarily, but in the long run, it causes bitterness and resentment. It destroys romantic love in your marriage.

Desires should be discussed, and both spouses should be willing to work and grow toward fulfilling them for the well-being of the relationship and the pleasure of God. But demanding turns good desires into something unhealthy and potentially sinful. It changes a beautiful and beneficial thing into something ugly and hurtful.

I will say more about expectations later, but for now let me suggest that the Apostle Paul defined "needs" as food and clothing (1 Tim. 6:8). Jesus clearly explained that the responsibility for meeting our needs falls on our heavenly Father (Matt. 6:31-32). When we look to another person to meet needs that only our heavenly Father can meet, we try to get things from our mate they are not designed for and create unnecessary drains on our marital resources. The psalmist wrote: ...*My expectations shall be of God...* (Psalm 62:5). When we look to our heavenly Father as the great Need-Meeter, we understand that He knows what we need before we ask Him (Matt. 6:8). When we understand that personal soul-stewardship requires accepting responsibility for the condition of our souls, then we will have a better perspective on our situation. We can then approach solutions from a Biblical perspective and please the Lord in the process.

Disappointments are part of every marriage. How you respond when your spouse disappoints you reveals something about you. Are your expectations from the Lord or from your spouse? If your spouse lets you down, can you communicate with her respectfully? Can you bring that disappointment to the Lord and find a sense of peace, yet continue to love her?

The Bible is rich in *one another* passages. Even a brief New Testament study of these "one another" passages will help provide the framework for living a life of love.

Disrespect

At first glance, it seems possible to fake respect. The right choice of words (Thank You, You're right. I'm sorry) can give the appearance of respect. However, eventually what is in the heart will become obvious. A wife may say, "I do respect you!" following her husband's complaint. But he knows whether her statement is true or not. When honesty bleeds through pretention (usually in a moment of anger), the words that flow through the lips reveal disrespect.

James warns his readers about the power of words: *Even so the tongue is a little member and boasts great things. See how great a forest a little fire kindles! And the tongue is a fire, a world of iniquity. The tongue is so set among our members that it defiles the whole body, and sets on fire the course of nature; and it is set on fire by hell* (James 3:5). Disrespectful statements can stir up a fire that can unnecessarily destroy a good relationship.

Jesus explained that whatever comes out of the mouth comes from the heart: *A good man out of the good treasure of his heart brings forth good; and an evil man out of the evil treasure of his heart brings forth evil. For out of the abundance of the heart his mouth speaks* (Luke 6:45).

These two passages highlight a common problem that must be identified: whether verbal or non-verbal, disrespect is a heart problem. The biggest hurdle to overcoming disrespect (or any heart issue) is to acknowledge the real problem. If you are unsure, a simple question may be adequate. Ask your spouse, "Do you feel respect from me?" If we view our behavior honestly and in light of God's Word, we will be in a better position to address our heart issues.

Disrespect (judging) is revealed in the way you think. Thinking you (or your ways) are better, smarter, or more important than your spouse reveals a problem with disrespect. When you forcefully impose your opinion on another person, without regard to how you may impact that person, you show great disrespect. Even if your judgment is correct, a disrespectful attitude creates unnecessary expenses for your marital resource.

Sinful Anger

Anger's most famous reputation is the shouting, red-faced, almost hateful vengeance version. And in many cases anger does show itself this way. The subtler form of anger is passivity. On the surface, it seems that being quiet and refusing to engage another person is a more loving and mature response. Although the external reaction is less obvious, the internal anger is just as destructive as its counterpart.

Passive anger is a silent killer. It operates covertly, but at its core, passivity is as violent and intentional as aggressive anger.

Whichever form of anger characterizes you, uncontrolled and unmanaged anger will inevitably cause problems in your relationship and cost you resources.

Anger is defined as *a feeling of great displeasure, hostility, indignation, or exasperation* (American Heritage Dictionary).

Elaine tells the story of how anger personally affected her and how it affected our relationship:

"I grew up with four siblings. I learned how to use angry outbursts to survive. Whoever was the loudest and the most passionate was the one who was heard. I developed some bad habits in expressing my anger. When I came to Christ, at the age of fifteen, I realized that using unhealthy expressions of anger to get my way and intimidate others needed to change. By God's grace, my angry outbursts have almost totally disappeared. I still get angry, but I have learned through the years how to communicate my anger in healthy ways.

Tim and I established rules for communication in our home such as no name calling, no derogatory statements, and no yelling. Angry outbursts are not allowed—by me or anyone in our family. I remember telling my children when they were very young, 'You can speak to me the way I speak to you.' That brought a lot of accountability to me."

While Elaine's struggle with expressing anger was outward, mine was inward. I was a stuffer. Instead of getting into a fight, I would give the appearance of cooperating and later take it out on Elaine in passive ways. To avoid conflict, I would not tell her when she had offended me. Instead of lovingly confronting her and expressing to her how her actions or words offended me, I would hold a grudge against her for "treating me badly."

For years, I did not realize how destructive this sinful way of handling anger was. When I realized how selfish and unloving passivity was, I was grieved. I began learning how to communicate appropriately. I determined to abandon passivity and in its place, choose responsible and Biblical ways of managing my emotions. Habits, maintained for many years, do not change easily. Their roots are deep and uprooting them requires hard work and consistency.

All anger is not sinful. In fact, we are instructed to "be angry" but not to sin. Mishandling anger can drain your marital resources quickly. Being quick-tempered (easily angered) is not a characteristic of love (1 Cor. 13:4-8).

Dishonesty (keeping secrets)

I have no greater joy than to hear that my children walk in truth (3 John 1:4).

Trust is based on truth and honesty. Keeping secrets from a spouse is a "red flag" in a relationship. Whether the secret involves practical matters like finances, schedules, facts about a business trip or subtler things like being dishonest about your feelings and opinions, secrets tear away at trust in your marriage.

A spouse who is a people-pleaser may struggle with honesty because he or she fears being rejected or disapproved of. A husband who struggles with purity may not want his wife to know he struggles. A wife who spends more than she should may not want to disclose it to her husband.

There may be times when you are not aware of why you treat your spouse the way you sometimes do. For example, the husband who becomes defensive when his wife brings to his attention something she would like him to change, may not realize the truth behind his defensiveness. He may argue that his wife is being critical or nagging. The truth may be that he feels a sense of failure and cannot admit his weaknesses.

Walking in truth can be progressive. As we mature, we better understand the truth about God, ourselves, and others. We are to walk in the truth (the light) that we currently have. The more truth we realize, the more freedom and joy we will experience.

Our struggle with telling the truth (or being accurate about facts) goes back to the Garden (Gen. 3). After Adam and Eve sinned by eating the forbidden fruit, they immediately covered themselves and hid from God. You and I experience the same temptation to hide when we feel shame.

Our capacity to lie (cover the truth) can be seen in the early years of child development. No one teaches a three-year-old to lie. He figures it out on his own. It is in his nature. By the time we become adults (who knows when that is!), we have learned to be very skillful at covering up and deceiving. It is a mature person who sees the virtue and value in speaking the truth in love (Eph. 4:15). When secrets are kept from a spouse, mistrust and suspicion abound, and needed marital resources are wasted on unnecessary offenses and misunderstanding.

One reason we choose to cover the truth is to protect ourselves. A husband may withhold an unpleasant doctor's report from his wife. He tells himself it is to protect her. A wife may choose not to tell her husband about an overdraft of their checking account. A person may withhold his opinion for fear of being criticized.

The Apostle Paul writes: *...we should no longer be children...but, speaking the truth in love, may grow up in all things into Him...* (Eph. 4:14-15). Here the Apostle couples speaking the truth with maturity. Reading on, he gives the practical reason for speaking the truth: *we are members of one another.* In marriage, a husband and wife are a team! What happens to one, happens to the other. You are in covenant with each other.

Oneness in marriage requires authenticity. Allowing the real you to emerge is necessary for marital intimacy. The truth is, you and I are flawed. And these flaws show up in marriage more than in any other relationship.

Be careful in handling the past! It's not uncommon for a husband or wife to recall an experience which took place prior to their marriage which they feel needs to be acknowledged. It may be something that happened *to you.* You may have been taken advantage of, abused, or neglected. Often, someone who was abused in childhood doesn't recall the events in adulthood. Or, it may be something you contributed to such as an abortion, an affair, or some other "skeleton" in your past that needs to be addressed.

The truth sets us free! (John 8:32). It frees us from the power of the unknown. It frees us from potential rejection and the horrifying question: "If they really knew me, would they accept me?" Freedom does not mean there won't be consequences or pain attached to the acknowledgement. It simply means that, in the end, freedom will accompany truth telling.

Bad Habits (especially if they've been brought to your attention)

We are devoted to the way we are. There is a certain loyalty we attach to our habits. In most cases, a person does not realize this attachment until he attempts to change.

Habits come in every size and shape. It may be that nail biting, burping at the table, leaving your dirty socks on the floor, and a hundred other things seemed to be an accepted fixture in your life before you were married. For you, these are normal and harmless. For your spouse, these habits can be irritating at the very least and offensive at worst!

A growing marriage demands change. The person who thinks he will get married and not need to change will be very disappointed. The one-flesh marriage relationship is intended to bring about a new entity which has never existed before. God will use your spouse to bring about changes He desires for you. The up-close-and-personal nature of marriage reveals, better than any other, how we impact others.

A simple example of how bad habits impact a marriage took place in the first months of our marriage. I worked at our family owned mechanic shop. It was not uncommon for me to come home with oil and grease on my clothes. My habit was to take my pants off inside-out. This habit was apparently okay with my mom, but Elaine didn't see the point. She politely asked if, when I removed my pants, I would leave the pant legs out. Then she wouldn't need to put her hand inside those dirty pants. It was a reasonable request. However, I kept forgetting. She was patient and would ask me to pull the pant leg out. Eventually, I changed my habit.

Some habits create unnecessary offenses and hurt feelings. When you become aware of a behavior that is offensive to your mate, you must be proactive in seeking to change. Some habits are easier to change than others. A fair amount of counseling is spent on helping people replace destructive habits with Christ-like habits. I have found that patience, on the part of both partners, is helpful. As long as the offended spouse knows that the other is trying, there seems to be a good amount of tolerance. A spouse can be gracious if the other is aware of the habit and sincerely wants to change. However, when an offensive behavior has been discussed and the offending spouse if fully aware of how his or her behavior offends the other and does not pursue change, tolerance diminishes and marital resources are quickly depleted.

Inconsiderateness, at the least, is at the root of habitual behavior that is not addressed. You risk deeper offenses by being insensitive to your spouse's feelings and requests. I remember an incident that took place at a wedding. While walking from the church to the reception area, I overheard the bride ask the groom, "Please don't smash the wedding cake in my face?" Her voice hinted of fear. The groom assured her that he would not do such a thing. To her dismay, when cake eating time came, the groom smashed the wedding cake in her face. She was devastated! As though that was not offensive enough, he turned toward a group of his single buddies and they all laughed.

Regardless of the reason you continue in a bad habit, if it is offensive to your spouse or to God, you cannot afford to continue. It is an Unnecessary Expense to your relationship. Unless you change, you will end up bankrupt.

Conflict over Parenting Issues

Unfortunately, many couples who marry have little or no preparation before saying "I Do." A candid discussion about important topics like parenting philosophies and child training rarely takes place.

When a child is added to a family, there are many issues that must be discussed. Otherwise, one parent leads out assuming the other agrees. Potentially, the couple is divided when it comes to standards of behavior, character development goals, table manners, bedtime, etc.

Parenting conflicts are common to all couples with children. Therefore, this is an area of your relationship that you cannot afford to ignore. There are no easy steps to unity when it comes to parenting. A husband and wife must go item by item through the varied list of situations surrounding training a child. Passivity, apathy, manipulation, or force is no way of establishing family standards. You and your spouse must do the hard work it takes to come up with a plan of discipline and training with which you are both comfortable and committed to.

Everything about effective parenting is dependent upon teamwork. You come up with your plan as a team. You implement the plan as a team. Then you figure out if this is the best approach and make adjustments as a team. God's Word is filled with Biblical principles to help you parent successfully. A good beginning project is to do a study on Biblical parenting.

Flirting

When a husband or wife feels awkward about how the other interacts with someone of the opposite sex, it is not uncommon to bring this to the spouse's attention. Whether it is jealously or simply wanting his or her mate to be more careful, the complaint is worth noting. If it is ignored, it can become an Unnecessary Expense for your relationship.

Flirting can be innocent and unintentional. Other flirting is obvious, although it may simply be a bad habit. You may have an outgoing and friendly personality that draws attention from others. This may be beneficial to you in the business world or other social settings. However, your spouse may detect (before you) when interactions with the opposite gender are inappropriate or potentially sending the wrong message.

Confiding in someone of the opposite sex, who is not your spouse, is a recipe for trouble. You may think, "We are only friends!" However, many affairs have taken place with a spouse's best friend. Neither ever intended it to happen. But they became so comfortable with each other, they failed to protect their hearts and their marriages.

It's not rocket science. Spending time alone, and in too much conversation, with someone other than your spouse can create an emotional bond that draws you away from your mate. No one thinks it could happen to them. After having an affair, a wife explained, "I always looked at women who did this and thought, "I would *never* do that'!"

The Apostle Paul wisely wrote: *let him who thinks he stands take heed lest he fall* (1 Cor. 10:12). The best remedy for not falling is knowing that you can.

If you are in a relationship that makes your spouse feel uncomfortable or insecure, do not ignore their concern. Put some distance between you and that person for the well-being of your relationship. Flirting, emotionally bonding, and confiding in someone of the opposite sex are things your marriage cannot afford.

Spending too much time away from Home

Getting away with friends is a great addition to a healthy marriage. Guys need "guy time" and girls need "girl time." However, too much time away from home can present unnecessary liabilities for your marital resources.

The way we spend our time reveals what we prioritize. People who have a hard time saying "no" can easily and unnecessarily burden themselves and their marriage. I have seen marriages on the brink of divorce simply because one spouse could not say "no." She told her husband he was more important than her mom, but when push came to shove, she gave in to her mom's requests. A husband said he really loved his wife and wanted to spend less time at work, yet, when his boss asked him to work late again, he just couldn't tell him "no."

If you are prone to letting things and people crowd your relationship, acknowledge it and be willing to make changes that will add to your relationship. Make yourself accountable to someone and refuse to make excuses when you fail.

Personal Weakness

"This is just the way I am. If you don't like it, tough!" Unfortunately, this is a common attitude in marriage. Character flaws cannot stay hidden in the close quarters of a marriage relationship. Pre-married couples may be able to cover their weaknesses prior to marriage, but it doesn't take long for personal weaknesses to emerge. Things like jealousy, pride, fear, lust, and self-centeredness have a way of showing up at the most inconvenient times.

Any sinful behavior or attitude that affects your marriage will demand resources from you and your spouse that you may not be able to afford. Do not be surprised if the Lord uses your spouse to bring to light things in you that He wants to change. Regardless of how prepared you may have been when you entered marriage, changes and adjustments are required.

Fear, anxiety, and stress place a tremendous burden on a relationship. Those who struggle in this area may avoid situations that pose the potential for anxiety by controlling their schedules. If you dislike crowds, you may avoid them. However, due to the "opposites attract" theory, you may have married someone who loves crowds. Thus, you have a dilemma. Will you nurture your personal weakness or choose to grow?

Personal weaknesses come in many forms. One person says, "I'm not a good communicator." Another says, "I don't like following orders." Personal weaknesses create marriage problems. The person who views the revealing of their weakness as an opportunity to grow will generate Marital Income. The person who refuses to address his weakness will not only miss the opportunity to grow, he will risk making unnecessary withdrawals.

The spirit of a man is the lamp of the LORD, searching all the inner depths of his heart (Prov. 20:27). The Lord searches every heart and tests those whom He loves (Jer. 17:10). He doesn't reveal our flaws to criticize us. He reveals them to replace them with His character. Jesus promised that, when the Holy Spirit came, He would guide us into all truth (Jn. 16:13). We all have blind spots, those things about ourselves of which we are not aware. Sometimes the Lord will use another person to reveal our blind spots. Many times, He will use your spouse.

When this happens, our pride propels us to deny what our spouse is saying. It is self-protection. Our weaknesses being seen by another person makes us feel vulnerable. It feels like someone else has control over us. Instead of allowing this process to play out, we abort it to avoid feeling out-of-control. Knowing that the Lord is guiding you toward growth and change can be comforting. Remember, your mate is not your enemy. The Lord may have revealed your weakness to her to move you toward intimacy.

Controlling

Some people are able to recognize and acknowledge their tendency to want to control others and circumstances. They are well on their way to entering the Change Process (Eph. 4:20-24). The person who wants to control people and things, but is unaware of this tendency, needs a little self-awareness.

Some people micro manage. And this can create problems in a relationship. One husband described his frustration toward his wife like this, "She polices me! It's like she watches everything I do and makes comments about it." A well-meaning wife may want to mother her husband. Of course, she may not realize she's doing this. Or, a well-meaning husband interacts with his wife as a father with his daughter, telling her how to do things and questioning her. It may seem caring, but many times, it conveys the message that the parented spouse cannot function properly without the help of the parenting spouse.

This issue of control is not always easy to identify. It can camouflage itself as being responsible. Usually, the spouse who is being controlled is quicker to identify the problem than is the spouse doing the controlling. Although a controlling spouse means well, they can come across as overbearing, smothering, and manipulative.

Allowing your spouse to be himself or herself and experience consequences for their actions can be difficult, especially when those consequences affect the spouse who is aware of the problem. An important factor that helps in relinquishing control is realizing that God is involved in the process. Without this awareness, we take matters into our hands without considering what the Lord may be doing in our spouse's life.

Be careful. Don't assume the role of God. He is much better at changing people than you and me.

In-Law Interference

God places the lonely in families...- Psalm 68:6

Family is a wonderful gift from the Lord. Children, parents, in-laws, and grandchildren can bring variety and fun to life. I have seen God's grace displayed more in my family relationships than any other. When I was a teen and unaware of God's love, I never would have dreamt that I would have such a wonderful wife and such lovely daughters, sons-in-law and grandchildren!

Family relationships don't always bring out the positive in us. Sometimes family members create unnecessary expenses for our marriage. Family members do not always see things from the same perspective. A concerned mom may freely speak her mind to her newly married son in an attempt to help. She may not even be aware of the pressure she is placing on him to have to choose between the loyalty he has toward her and his wife.

Therefore, shall a man leave his father and his mother, and shall cleave unto his wife: and they shall be one flesh (Genesis 2:18). The two-fold process of leaving and cleaving begins with a decision, but it must be practically lived out. For many couples, the failure to leave creates problems with cleaving. Cleaving does not happen automatically and sometimes it is complicated. Sometimes the difficulty is due to parents who don't let go easily. Other times, it is the adult child who cannot seem to let go of the support of his or her parents.

Jen and James discovered how difficult the transition from singleness to marriage can be. Jen's parents had always made sure Jen was provided for. They paid for her college tuition and expenses, bought her clothes, and recently bought her a car a year before she married James.

James had worked his way through college and had very little to spare. He learned to do without at times, since his parents weren't in a position to help. In addition to Jen have difficulty adjusting to her new lifestyle, her parents were compelled to "help out" Jen and James. The help was welcomed by Jen, but James was having a problem with it. He felt like he and Jen needed to establish their new life together with what they had instead of being dependent on Jen's parents.

This created problems between Jen and James. It also created problems between James and his in-laws. He tried to communicate with Jen's dad, but he took offense to James' concern.

James and Jen had many conversations about the importance of leaving and cleaving. They discussed how the Lord was their provider and they needed to depend upon Him and each other.

In time, James and Jen were able to distinguish themselves as a separate family. Eventually, Jen's parents were able to give them gifts and even financial blessings. But Jen and James understood that these were simply blessings to be appreciated, not resources to be dependent upon.

Many well intentioned parents unintentionally create Unnecessary Expenses for their adult sons and daughters. If you are facing in-law interference in your marriage, you will need to discuss how you, as a couple, need to establish your separate identity as a family. Loving confrontation and a few well established boundaries can get you moving in the right direction.

Financial Irresponsibility

Financial Irresponsibility is a huge Unnecessary Expense in marriage. How you handle money, the value you place on it, and the trust you give it needs to be assessed through the Biblical lens. How you prioritize money says a lot about what is important to you. In many marriages (maybe because opposites attract), there will a spender and a saver. One spouse may take great care over the management of finances while the other has no clue where the money comes from or goes. An irresponsible spender, especially if the spending is a way of coping with life's pressures, can bring plenty of Unnecessary Expenses into a marriage relationship. Impulsive buying, poor management, and increasing debt contribute to the tendency for a spender to hide information and thereby break trust with a spouse. I will say more about this when we talk about Marital Debt. For now, you will do well to educate yourself in money management. Learning how to give, save, and manage your income and expenses can go a long way in getting rid of this Unnecessary Marital Expense.

Unrealistic Expectations

You cannot avoid having expectations in marriage. In fact, some expectations are expected (no pun intended). A husband and wife should keep the promises they made when they entered into the marriage covenant. A wife should expect her husband to love her, be faithful to her, and provide for her and the family. A husband should expect his wife to support and respect him, and love and nurture the children, if and when they come along.

Some expectations are appropriate. Others need to be assessed. A wife may expect her husband to bring his dirty clothes to the laundry room or to wash the car when it needs it. A husband may expect his wife to be considerate of his fishing tackle and understand that he needs a weekend away every now and then. Many of these expectations come from our family of origin.

Disappointments, like expectations, cannot be avoided either. When you expect someone to meet a certain standard of behavior and he or she doesn't, you experience disappointment. Your expectations may be realistic (A husband can learn to communicate his feelings. A wife can learn to communicate more logically). However, when the expectations placed on a person are unrealistic, the outcome is more than simply disappointment. It is anger, confusion, and bitterness. A young bride marries a man and expects he will be like her dad or some other guy she respects. She may expect him to fix things when they break, care for the animals the way her dad did, and a long list of other things that have never been identified. A husband may expect his new bride to cook like his mom, clean the house, make his bed, and make his doctor appointments the way his mom did. He may expect her to be a stay at home mom and a thrifty coupon shopper. It is important for this couple to discuss their expectations.

How you react to unfulfilled expectations says a lot about you and what you believe. Good communication is vital when it comes to finding common ground on expectations. Be patient, communicate clearly, seek to understand, and be willing to help your spouse grow. There will, no doubt, be things about your spouse that you will have to accept. You will need to seek the Lord about your attitude and expectations.

Misunderstanding Conflict

Conflict paves the path to Intimacy. - Author unknown

It is said that opposites attract. With time, opposites may attack! The wife who used to appreciate her husband's easy going, laidback approach to life now sees it as irresponsibility. The husband who once appreciated his wife's talent for organization and order now sees it as control and manipulation. She once thought of her husband as a good listener. Now she sees him as non- engaging and passive. He once loved his wife's ability to talk for hours on end. Now he sees her as nagging and domineering.

The love that once was blind now sees in full color! This couple's differences create opportunity for conflict. I mentioned earlier in this book that volatile conflict which is destructive and in no way beneficial should be avoided. The conflict I refer to here is the clashing differences that can actually benefit a marriage, if the conflict is handled appropriately. This healthy kind of conflict in marriage is normal and unavoidable. We read in Proverbs 27:17: *As iron sharpens iron, so a friend sharpens a friend.* The word "sharpens" comes from a word that means to be *fierce* or *severe*. If you have ever sharpened a lawnmower blade with a grinder or seen it done, you know how intense and heated the sharpening process can be.

God uses conflict to teach us. A saying Elaine and I have adopted (but cannot remember who said it) is: *Conflict paves the path to Intimacy.* When a couple successfully moves through conflict to resolution, they develop a stronger bond. Researchers have found that "two-thirds of unhappily married spouses who stayed married reported that their marriages were happy five years later. In addition, the most unhappy marriages reported the most dramatic turnarounds: among those who rated their marriages as very unhappy, almost eight out of ten who avoided divorce were happily married five years later."[9] The study went on to say that one of the contributing factors of these couples' success was their commitment to make their marriage work. This factor alone has the potential to propel individuals toward solution-based approaches.

Bitterness and Resentment

I remember my confusion the day I realized that I didn't understand my wife. I had returned from an exhausting day of work. Elaine was folding clothes. She had been reading a book on marriage that day. It seemed to me that every time she read one of those books, I would be in trouble. After asking her how her day went, she proceeded to tell me some of the things she had been reading: how a husband was supposed to love his wife, listen to her, understand her, etc. I listened carefully but when she started repeating the things she had already said, I turned away, mid-sentence, and said, "You already said that!" and I walked out the room. (I now know that was a bad idea.) I walked into the family room and pulled the Bible off the bookshelf (thinking I would be the spiritual one in the argument). I opened it to the book of Colossians, and my eyes went directly to verse 9 of chapter 1. "*Husbands, love your wives and do not grow bitter toward them.*"

I learned two things that day: First, I did not understand my wife. I did not understand why she was upset, why she thought differently from me, and why she processed circumstances differently. Secondly, because I did not understand her, I was growing bitter toward her. The Apostle Peter's words went through my mind, *likewise, husbands, live with your wives in an understanding way, showing honor to the woman as the weaker vessel, since they are heirs with you of the grace of life, so that your prayers may not be hindered* (1 Pet. 3:7).

Resentment is defined as "a feeling of indignant displeasure or persistent ill will".[10] Resentment is a consequence of not addressing conflict or offenses appropriately. The Bible describes bitterness as acrid or pungent (James 3:14), which is distasteful, corrosive, and repulsive. Bitterness will erode love in your marriage. If your true feelings toward your spouse are bitter and resentful, you are leaving a gaping hole in your Marital reservoir.

Work on Your Marriage Budget (Individual Worksheet)

Go to your Individual *Marriage Budget Worksheet* (Appendix A) and list any Unnecessary Expenses that are current in your marriage. Be careful to first list the items that you are responsible for and not those of your mate's. For example, if your spouse is irresponsible with finances, place this item at the bottom of your list. You may have the opportunity to share these items with your spouse later. Hopefully, he or she will also list those items on his or her worksheet. For now, concentrate on how you have personally contributed to the problem though Unnecessary Expenses. Later, you and your spouse can work together on your combined *Marriage Budget Worksheet*. You can find a summary of Common Unnecessary Expenses Appendix E.

Join the conversation on Facebook. Share how this chapter has been beneficial to you.

https://www.facebook.com/managingyourmarriage

Chapter 5
Marital Debt

Marital Debt is any issue in your marriage that has not been resolved but is still requiring resources.

The Bible is clear when it comes to keeping your word. *When you make a vow to God, do not delay to pay it; for He has no pleasure in fools. Pay what you have vowed-better not to vow than to vow and not pay* (Ecclesiastes 5:4-5). The Apostle Paul writes: *Render therefore to all their due, taxes to whom taxes are due, customs to whom customs, fear to whom fear, honor to whom honor. Owe no one anything except to love one another...* (Romans 13:7-8).

Marital Debt is the principal cause of divorce. Marital Debt is any issue in your marriage that has not been resolved and is still requiring current resources. Marital Debt can arise from at least two sources: *Personal Debt, past or current,* is an obstacle to the health of the marriage. This may include a poor response to tragic or painful experiences that only one spouse encounters, but is affecting the marriage and *Unresolved Issues* due to one spouse offending the other.

Personal debt is an unresolved personal issue which inevitably affects the marriage relationship. Everyone brings personal debt into their marriage. For some, personal debt is a past abortion that has never been addressed. For others, it is childhood physical or sexual abuse. Personal debt can be any past experience that is still affecting you negatively and demanding emotional resources. This could include bitterness over something you are still hurt and angry about, yet have not been able to forgive. It could be the inability to trust another person or any number of barriers that interfere with the health of your marriage

These unaddressed issues create obstacles in a relationship and usually cause marital problems. Until these are addressed properly, they will continue to steal your personal and relational resources.

Marital Debt is all-consuming. It creates walls of division between you and your spouse and hinders the flow of life and freshness in your relationship.

Each person reacts to negative situations differently. Even though God's Word gives us hope and help, many of us continue to default to old coping skills that are deeply ingrained and not productive. Some of these coping skills may have worked fairly well while you were single. However, marriage places you in a different environment, and you may find that your old coping skills do not work in your marriage. For example, if someone offended you when you were single, you may have simply rejected that person, marked him off your friend list, and burned that relationship bridge. (Of course, this method is not Biblical and it really did not work for you. It only seemed to work.) In marriage, when your spouse offends you, you cannot use your old methods of dealing with offenses. Rejecting your spouse when you are offended not only does not work, but it creates more relational problems. You will have to learn new ways of dealing with offenses.

Personal Debt

> ...the LORD'S hand is not shortened, that it cannot save; nor His ear heavy, that it cannot hear. But your iniquities have separated you from your God; and your sins have hidden His face from you, so that He will not hear (Isaiah 59:1-2).

Sin creates division in any relationship. In this passage, the prophet explains that a broken relationship with God is not God's problem, but ours! It is because of our sin. The way we live and the choices we make can destroy unity in a relationship.

God has provided a remedy for personal debt—the cross. The gospel (good news) explains that Jesus bore our personal debt (our sin) in His body on the cross (Col. 2:14). All the things you and I have ever done to offend God—things that have created negative consequences in our lives—Jesus took upon Himself when He was nailed to the cross. The gospel offers a simple solution to our sin problem.

There are two things we must believe in order to be free from sin and its consequences. First, *we must believe and accept what God says about forgiveness.* Some people have a very difficult time forgiving themselves, even though God has graciously forgiven them. Past memories may linger and even torment a person who is regretful over his or her past sins. We must embrace what God says is true about our sin and His forgiveness. If you struggle with self-forgiveness and are still plagued with shame, you must choose to believe the truth. If God has forgiven you, stop punishing yourself and accept the freedom from sin He offers.

Secondly, *we must commit our lives to Jesus Christ and trust Him to lead us.* Each person must do this in his or her own heart. No one can do this for you. To successfully address personal debt, you can only do so by approaching Him through the way He has established.

Your story began *in the beginning* (Gen. 1:1). God created you to be an expression of Himself. Everything He created was good and for His pleasure. Life in the garden was sinless and in perfect harmony with God. Sin entered and opened the door for death and destruction (Rom. 5:12). When Adam and Eve sinned, they immediately experienced shame and fear. Guilt over what they had done and their disobedience left them feeling alone. They covered themselves and hid from God (Gen. 3:7-8).

You and I suffer the same consequences today as Adam and Eve did thousands of years ago. The sin that entered the human race, like a genetic fatal disease, has been passed down through the generations to you and me. There is only one remedy. The solution is found in the sacrificial life, death, and resurrection of Jesus Christ.

In the words of the Apostle Paul, *You were dead because of your sins and because your sinful nature was not yet cut away. Then God made you alive with Christ, for he forgave all our sins. He cancelled the record of the charges against us and took it away by nailing it to the cross* (Col. 2:13-14).

Anyone who places his trust in the work Jesus did on the cross receives forgiveness of sins and a new identity as a child of God (1 John 3:1). The cross solved the problem of sin that separated us from God. Personal debt is done away with when we come to God through Jesus Christ! We have been adopted into the family of God as His children!

For readers who have not made the decision to trust Jesus Christ, the following prayer is a good place to start:

Dear God, I recognize my need for You in my life. I turn my life over to You. Please forgive me for my many sins, and accept me in Your mercy. I accept the Truth of Your Word that You sent Christ to die for me so that I could be in a right relationship with You. Please take Your rightful place as Lord in my life. I make this request in the Name of Jesus Christ, Amen.

Marriage and God

Although many couples enter marriage without an awareness or interest in God, when we look at God's design for marriage in Scripture, we see a purpose far greater than personal benefits. He created the marriage covenant for His purposes and pleasure. Embracing God's design for your life and marriage requires the realization that sin has separated you from Him and that Jesus Christ is your hope and God's solution for restoring that relationship. Without a personal and practical relationship with God, you cannot be truly restored in your relationship with your spouse. Shame, guilt, and everything that drains life from you will affect your relationship. Jesus Christ frees us (releases) us from our sin debt.

Marital Debt

Perhaps the best way to understand *Marital Debt* is to look at it as unresolved offenses. In the previous chapter, we looked at Unnecessary Expenses. If these are not addressed appropriately, they can create deep personal offenses which repeatedly show up in present conflicts.

For example, a seemingly harmless comment can connect to past offenses that ignite negative reactions. The statement, by itself, would not normally evoke such passionate reactions, but because it is "more of the same" offense, it triggers all that is connected to it. In this case, we have the proverbial "straw that breaks the camel's back."

When husbands and wives continue in behaviors or habits (Unnecessary Expenses) that are offensive to their mates, these become long term debts that will continually drain current resources from the relationship. Let's take a look at some of the common debts in marriage.

Offenses

> *An offended friend is harder to win back than a fortified city. Arguments separate friends like a gate locked with bars* (Prov. 18:19 - NLT)

Offenses come in varied degrees. Some offenses are easier to get over than others. When offenses are deep and personal, they create huge obstacles in a relationship. As in the above verse, an offended party may surround himself with such a protective barrier, it is almost impossible to penetrate. Let us take a brief look at offenses from the broader perspective.

The word "offended" comes from a Hebrew word (*pasha*) that means to sin or rebel against. In most cases, this Hebrew word is translated *transgress*. Thus, to offend someone is to sin against them, and thereby cause them harm.

We find two general types of offenses in Scripture. One type of offense is a *legitimate offense*. A legitimate offense causes the offended party to alter his or her life. It has such a powerful effect upon the offended one, that the offense becomes a stumbling block in his or her path. The one offended just can't seem to recover from it. The other is a chosen offense which does not necessarily have the power to alter your life. It is a *perceived offense*. In this case, a person chooses to take offense.

An example of a *legitimate offense* is found in Jesus' warning about children: *It would be better for him if a millstone were hung around his neck, and he were thrown into the sea, than that he should offend one of these little ones* (Luke 17:2). Here, the word *offend* means *trip up, stumble* or *entice to sin*. The word picture is one of a person hiding in the church pews and stretching his leg to trip the person walking down the aisle. This person did not see it coming. He was blind-sided and given cause to stumble. We see a similar example in the Apostle Paul's instructions to the Corinthians concerning a weaker brother. Regarding eating foods that may offend, he says, *...when you thus sin against the brethren, and wound their weak conscience, you sin against Christ. Therefore, if food makes my brother stumble, I will never again eat meat, lest I make my brother stumble* (1 Cor.8:10-13). Here, the connection is clearly made between offending and sinning against the weaker brother.

Jesus taught his disciples how to handle offenses. He said, *if your brother sins against you, go and tell him his fault between you and him alone. If he hears you, you have gained your brother* (Matt. 18:15). When an offense occurs, the offender may or may not know that he has offended the other person. Thus Jesus tells His disciples to *tell him his fault*. The implication is that the person may not be aware that he has offended you. By *telling him his fault*, you love him enough to help him, and protect your heart from holding a grudge (Lev. 19:17-18). Also, there is the hope that loving confrontation will lead to a restored relationship (Matt. 18:15).

A *perceived offense* is unnecessary or without good reason. This type of offense is especially unnecessary when the offender does not realize he or she is offending.

Here is an example of *a perceived offense*. After Jesus lovingly confronted the Pharisees about their hypocrisy, the disciples asked Him, *"Do You know that the Pharisees were offended when they heard this saying?"* But He answered and said, *"Every plant which My heavenly Father has not planted will be uprooted. Let them alone. They are blind leaders of the blind. And if the blind leads the blind, both will fall into a ditch"* (Matt. 15:1-14).

Jesus' response seems odd. Why did He not try to "clear the air," pursue unity and restore the relationship? We can only speculate, but the implication seems clear. What Jesus told the Pharisees was not only true, but it was for their benefit. They were blind to their true need, so Jesus lovingly revealed their true condition. Instead of seeing the truth, they resisted agreeing with God about their sin. Because they were not open and receptive to the things He said, they *chose* to be offended. Since their offense was of their own choosing, Jesus concluded, *Let them alone.* It seems Jesus did not assume responsibility for their poor choices.

There is also the case of an *adopted offense.* An adopted offense is when one person, who was not directly sinned against, adopts the offense of another. For example, your brother-in-law speaks rudely to your sister. Your sister's offense may be legitimate, and you may genuinely empathize with her. Even though your brother-in-law did not directly offend you, you adopt your sister's offense and therefore change the way you relate to your brother-in-law.

You and I must be careful to steward our souls. We must guard our hearts from unnecessary offenses. When we are offended, we must assume personal responsibility in the matter. *"Be on your guard! If your brother sins, rebuke him; and if he repents, forgive him* (Luke 17:3).

Now, let us look at some of the offenses that create Marital Debt.

Common Debts In Marriage
Broken Trust

Broken trust is the over-arching consequence of relational offenses. Marriage is built on trust. In the context of covenant, trust is assumed and expected in marriage and provides security and a sense of safety. Offenses like lying, deceitfulness, infidelity, affairs (whether they are physical or only emotional), and sexual offenses (whether it is pornography or selfish demands in the bedroom) are destructive to a marriage relationship and create Marital Debt.

The feeling of betrayal that accompanies broken trust can be overwhelming. Confusion, fear, and uncertainty cause a relationship to stop in its tracks. In many cases, the offender does not realize or accept the awful pain he or she has inflicted on the other person. Broken trust is by far the hardest debt to pay off in marriage. Later in this chapter, I will address how you and your spouse can work at rebuilding trust.

Financial Irresponsibility

John opened several credit card accounts and made purchases which reached the maximum. Jean was totally unaware until the creditors started calling and demanding payment. He could no longer hide. He was forced to disclose some of the financial chaos to Jean, but he told her only what was necessary to get over this hurdle. His other financial problems would eventually catch up with him, but he did not want to upset her any more than necessary.

Up to this point, Jean had trusted John completely. When he would explain how his "business deals" were doing well, she believed him. Even when Jean inquired about details, John assured her that everything was fine and she need not worry. When the truth came out, Jean was devastated and could no longer trust John.

Jean demanded that John accompany her to marriage counseling. They made several attempts and tried to work through their current crisis and the choices that led up to it. Unfortunately, John continued to hide things from Jean and ultimately their marriage ended. The relational debt John created was enormous and his refusal to be honest made rebuilding trust impossible.

Getting rid of Marriage Debt requires a lot of work. It requires true *repentance— a change of mind leading to a change of behavior.* If a spouse wants to save his or her marriage and rebuild trust, serious consideration must be given to his or her relationship with God. Personal debt must be addressed before any success can be realized in mending what has been broken. Without God's help, it will be impossible.

For more information about *The Repentance Process*, go to relationalimpact.com.

Spousal Abuse

Spousal abuse, whether it is physical, verbal, or emotional, is sinful and destructive. *Love does no harm* (Rom. 13:10). There is absolutely no place in marriage for abuse of any kind. Sadly, abuse is prevalent in marriage, even Christian marriages. I cannot adequately address the subject of abuse here, but I will point out that we, in our brokenness, are not always in a position to judge the depth of pain associated with abuse, especially when it is inflicted by someone we trust.

Mary was raised in a verbally abusive home. She and her family could send verbal bombs that could destroy a person without much effort. Name calling, belittling, and accusations to gain power over an opponent were just a few of the skills Mary learned growing up. Before she married Dan, she was able to keep much of her abusive tendencies at bay. However, after marriage, they emerged rather quickly. Dan wondered, "Who is this person? Where is this coming from?" Of course, Mary had excuses for her abusive language. Usually, she would blame Dan and something he did or said.

Dan felt the piercing of Mary's words deep within his soul. When he spoke to her about it, she minimized it and said he was making a big issue out of nothing. The continual offense of verbal abuse caused Dan to withdraw and disconnect from Mary. With every offense, the distance between them increased. In the beginning, Mary was unwilling to take responsibility for her destructive speech. However, she eventually recognized how her communication was affecting Dan and their children. The Lord convicted her and she was able to call her verbal abuse what it was—sin.

Mary acknowledged the powerful hold these verbal habits had on her. She humbly entered the Repentance Process. The Lord has done a great work in Mary, enabling her to use her speech to encourage and build up her husband and children. Dan was able to work on forgiveness toward Mary. Her humility and hard work toward change made forgiveness much easier for Dan.

Indifference and Apathy

Being indifferent or apathetic toward your spouse will inevitably create debt in your marriage. Holocaust survivor, Elie Wiesel, said, "The opposite of love is not hate, it's indifference." Indifference and apathy send very negative messages to your spouse. Instead of being committed to love, you choose an "I don't really care" attitude which leaves your spouse abandoned.

Love cares, even when it has to confront an uncomfortable situation. Love focuses on the well-being of the other person. Indifference and apathy provide a self-protective facade that is contrary to the nature of love.

When a wife reveals her heart to her husband, she needs validation. She needs to know that her husband cares about what is important to her. When he views her concerns as nonsense or irrelevant, she perceives him as being uncaring and unfeeling. Even when a husband disagrees with his wife and thinks she is totally wrong, he can care for her by lovingly speaking what is on his mind and helping his wife through her difficult situation.

Many wives have complained about their husbands misunderstanding their needs and trying to fix the situation. A common response from wives is: "I just want you to listen to me."

Many husbands fall to the temptation toward apathy when they become frustrated with their wives. A common complaint from husbands is: "I can't do anything to please her."

Years of indifference and apathy create emotional demands in a marriage that drains the couple of their relational resources. Indifference and apathy, like all offenses, must be acknowledged as sinful and repentance must be pursued.

Dishonesty

Lies come in many different shades and sizes. Some lies are overt and for intentional gain. Others are subtle and self-protective. I addressed dishonesty in Chapter Four (Unnecessary Expenses). Here, I want to address a subtle but common form of dishonesty in marriage—not speaking the truth in love.

To speak the truth in love implies that truth-telling is meant to benefit another person. The Apostle Paul suggests that truth-telling and maturity go hand in hand (Eph. 4:15). It is not uncommon for a spouse to conceal his or her true feelings. Whether this is done for self-protection or to avoid conflict, the result is the same—distrust and Marital Debt.

Fear of rejection (disapproval) and a sense of unworthiness (personal debt) can cause an insecure spouse to avoid being honest. The popular example is when a wife asks her husband, "How does this dress look on me?". One husband may grin while the other stands paralyzed by the question. To be fair, some husbands can be honest with their wives about such matters. Most, however, feel that a trap is being set and they want to avoid the question at all costs. A husband may not answer his wife truthfully for a number of reasons, but regardless, his wife wants the truth (in most cases). A husband may experience the equivalent of test-fright.

This scenario sounds innocent enough, but when subtle deception persists in a relationship, a false sense of security is created. When the true feelings and opinions of the insecure spouse are finally disclosed, the reality that the other spouse has lived a lie comes crashing in. Thus the relationship that once seemed healthy now seems full of deceit and untruths.

Sometimes people are dishonest because they are not fully aware or they are in denial. I was guilty of this. As I stated earlier, I had a lot of anger growing up. It wasn't until I was an adult that I realized this was true.

Growing up, my dad occasionally expressed anger is ways I didn't like. Somewhere along the way, I made an internal vow that I would never show anger outwardly. However, the pendulum swung to the other side. I stuffed my anger so deeply that I refused to acknowledge its presence. Elaine would ask, "Are you angry?" I would say, "No. I'm just irritated." I used other anger-light words like frustrated and aggravated. But I could not seem to bring myself to admit that *I was angry*. To me, anger was bad. It was wrong. It was something to be avoided.

There were times when Elaine would do or say something that upset me. Instead of lovingly confronting her and letting her know how she was impacting me, I would stuff the offense and become angry. The problem was, I wouldn't tell her. Of course she could tell that something was wrong. When she asked, "Are you upset about something?" I would lie and say "No. I'm just tired."

It wasn't until I came face-to-face with the little phrase *Be angry...* (Eph. 4:26) that I realized how big my problem was. It confused me. Why would God tell me to *be angry*? It stopped me in my tracks. For the first time, I realized that, although anger was something everyone experiences, I did not understand it and did not know how to manage it. The verse continues, *Be angry and do not sin* (Eph. 4:26). I had confused the idea of anger with its expression.

I slowly began to detect when I was becoming angry and would speak about it honestly. It was awkward in the beginning, as with any new endeavor. Without acknowledging the truth about myself and my anger, I would have never dealt with it appropriately. It would have continued to be a drain on our marital resources.

Infidelity

Merriam-Webster's dictionary defines *infidelity* as "unfaithfulness to a moral obligation." One of the synonyms is to be *treacherous*. The Bible speaks clearly to this matter in the book of Malachi. Here, the Lord is explaining why He was not answering the prayers of His people:

> ...*You cover the altar of the LORD with tears, with weeping and crying; So He does not regard the offering anymore, nor receive it with goodwill from your*

hands. Yet you say, "For what reason?" Because the LORD has been witness between you and the wife of your youth, with whom you have dealt treacherously; Yet she is your companion and your wife by covenant. 15 But did He not make them one, having a remnant of the Spirit? And why one? He seeks godly offspring. Therefore, take heed to your spirit, and let none deal treacherously with the wife of his youth. 16 "For the LORD God of Israel says That He hates divorce, for it covers one's garment with violence," Says the LORD of hosts. "Therefore take heed to your spirit, that you do not deal treacherously" (Mal. 2:13-16-NKJV).

This is a powerful warning against infidelity. The word translated *treacherously* means to "act covertly; to pillage: deal deceitfully or unfaithfully, to offend."

Other synonyms of infidelity are: *unfaithfulness, adultery, extramarital relations, extramarital sex; faithlessness, disloyalty, falseness, breach of trust, treachery, double-dealing, duplicity, deceit...* Thus, infidelity can certainly be sexual. But it can take place in other relational areas as well. Infidelity takes place when a person neglects to keep his or her marriage vows; i.e. go outside the marriage for desires intended to be fulfilled in marriage.

Sometimes infidelity is referred to as an *affair.* An affair implies one or more events where something specifically takes place. Certainly, this would include any type of sexual encounters one might have apart from his or her spouse. An affair can also be *emotional* in nature. According to a relationship expert, "Over half of all emotional affairs start out innocently as online friendships. More than 70 percent of those friendships or flirtations will end up as real time affairs..."[11]

Randy had just had a huge fight with Jessica. It ended with Jessica asking Randy to leave. She didn't want to see him again! Randy didn't know who to talk to, so he contacted his friend Jill "just to talk." He explained that Jill was easy to talk to. She seemed to understand him and didn't judge him the way Jessica did. Randy was warned by friends to not "get involved" with Jill. He became very upset that his friends would think there was anything going on between them. It wasn't very long before Randy decided to divorce Jessica. He was planning to marry Jill.

Emotional affairs develop subtly. It is not uncommon for a person being lured into an affair to deny it is happening. Like Randy, when the person is questioned, it will usually be denied.

The above passage from Malachi urges: *take heed to your spirit.* This means "to hedge about (as with thorns), i.e. guard; to protect and attend to." No one is exempt from potentially dealing treacherously with their spouse. One safeguard is to avoid sharing intimate details of your life with someone of the opposite sex, even if the person is a friend to both you and your spouse. Be wise. Guys, find another guy you trust who will give you wise counsel. Ladies, find a woman you can confide in who will give you Biblical advice. This is certainly a case for the older to teach the younger (Titus 2:1-6).

Sexual Offenses (Pornography and selfish demands)

Jason was introduced to pornography when he was 12. His friend's dad had a stash of magazines in one of their outbuildings, and Jason and his friends found more than enough time to visit the outbuilding. It wasn't long before Jason felt more comfortable being alone when he looked at porn.

Jason became a Believer in Jesus Christ in his senior year of High School. He hoped his porn-viewing would stop but it didn't. Even after he married Lori, he would find himself staying up late after she went to bed so he could visit a few websites. One day, Lori stumbled upon the sites Jason had been visiting. She was horrified! He was ashamed!

Jason and Lori are not alone in their story. The impact of pornography has taken its toll on many marriages. Many work through the difficulty of learning, growing in understanding, and forgiveness. For others, the shocking reality of a husband's or wife's secret is the proverbial nail in the coffin.

Many times, the involvement with pornography will pervert the thinking of its user. A husband may pressure his wife to do things in the bedroom that she feels very uncomfortable with.

Secrets and the dark downward spiral of pornography can create Marital Debt at the deepest level. God created us as sexual beings. When we function according to His design in the covenant of marriage, sex becomes an Income Source that perpetually grows. However, when we use sex for selfish reasons, we pervert God's original purpose for sex and end up "using" the person He gave instead of loving her or him.

Sexual offenses can be the most difficult to overcome and one of the largest debts to pay off in marriage. However, since *what is impossible with man is possible with God* (Matt. 19:26), God can use even the most painful situations to bring about good (Rom. 8:28). Pornography users must see the reality of their choices. Many times, like in Jason's case, there is long running relationship which has developed between the user and the object of choice. This relationship, along with its entrenched loyalties, must be addressed and broken.

When chronic bad habits go without repentance, they cause repetitive injury to the other person and create huge amounts of debt in a relationship. These unresolved offenses can continue for years and create walls between a husband and wife. These walls can become so high; they no longer see each other. They see a problem, not a person. The love and fondness that was once between them is now replaced by anger and disrespect. Neglected Marital Debt creates a huge amount of pain in a person and thus, in a marriage. There is no way to have a thriving, fulfilling, abundant marriage when you have unresolved debt.

Addressing Marital Debt

To gain insight into dealing with Marital Debt appropriately, let us again consider a financial budget. According to financial author Dave Ramsey, the best way to pay off credit card debt is to start with the smallest debt. By paying off the smallest debt first, you accomplish at least two things: 1) You have quick success, thus you are encouraged to tackle the larger debt and 2) you get experience being self-disciplined and intentional about paying off debt. The more successful you are in resolving small debt, the more likely you will be successful resolving larger debt.

The same is true when addressing Marital Debt. When you and your spouse agree to begin addressing your Marital Debt, choose a small debt that you both agree is a debt.

Sean and Katie both agreed that Sean's foul language directed at Katie when he would get angry was a large Marital Debt. Katie walked on eggshells whenever she perceived Sean was getting angry. The hurt inflicted by Sean's cutting words caused her to withdraw and feel very unsafe. They rarely ever had a successful conversation because Katie was afraid to be honest. This had been a long-term problem in their marriage and they were both eager to address it. However, their communication skills were not good enough to tackle such a large debt. They would need to start with something more manageable.

Sean and Katie agreed to address the more recent offense of Katie and Sean feeling unappreciated by the other. Both were weak on compliments and strong on criticism. With this issue agreed upon, they were now ready to learn some conflict resolution skills and pay off some Marital Debt.

With time and experience, Sean and Katie were eventually able to move beyond their Marital Debt and begin rebuilding trust. Because they started with smaller debt, they learned how to resolve conflict and were able to grow together.

Like Sean and Katie, as you are able to resolve small conflicts, you will gain experience applying the Biblical principles outlined below.

Preparation for Action

I want to suggest three components of preparation that will help you move toward addressing Marital Debt.

1. *A Biblical Mindset*: When approaching the task of resolving conflict and removing Marital Debt, it is important to have the *right motive*. Your primary motive should be to please the Lord and be obedient to Him. *And whatever you do, do it heartily, as to the Lord and not to men, knowing that from the Lord you will receive the reward of the inheritance; for you serve the Lord Christ* (Colossians 3:23). Each person must be careful to do what he or she is instructed to do from God's Word. If your spouse does the same, you will have an easier path toward reconciliation. If, however, your spouse does not respond the way you think he or she should, keep your focus on pleasing the Lord. You cannot force your spouse to do his or her part. You may be tempted to give up if she doesn't work as hard as you. Don't give in! Remember the words of the Lord Jesus to Peter, when he asked about John: *You follow Me* (John 21:22).

   A few things to remember as you consider resolving Marital Debt: 1. God is with you! He will not abandon you in your time of trouble (Ps. 46:1). 2. God is Sovereign! This is not a surprise to Him. He knew what was going to happen before it happened. He will not allow you to be tempted above what you are able to bear (1 Cor. 10:13). If a sparrow doesn't fall to the ground without the Father's permission (Matt. 10:29-GWT), surely you are not facing your circumstances alone. 3. This will turn out for your good! God uses even the most painful of circumstances to conform us to the Image of Christ (Rom. 8:28-31).

2. *Willingness to Sacrifice*: Another component necessary for paying off Marital Debt is the *willingness to sacrifice*. A person who is committed to paying off financial debt must sacrifice some of his present comfort for future benefits.

This requires paying close attention to details. Eventually, the sacrifices will pay off and he will be freed from debt!

The same is true for Marital Debt. You may have a mountain of problems that you have not dealt with for a number of years. But remember, the Lord blesses our efforts when we follow His Word and seek to please Him (Jam.1:25). Faith is acting like God tells the truth. He will enable you to do what you feel you are not able to do (Phil. 4:13). If you are willing, you will eventually be able to do what He desires you to do (Phil. 2:13).

He will work with you and for you as you lean heavily upon Him. When you have moments of discouragement, when you feel that resolving long-term Marital Debt is impossible, remember: *what is impossible with man is possible with God*! He is more committed to helping you resolve your marital conflicts than you are. Choose to love sacrificially and you will not fail (1 Cor. 13:8a).

3. *Commitment to the Process*: In addition to Biblical thinking and a willingness to love sacrificially, you will need to be committed to the process. The process through which you must go is designed to mature you (Rom. 5:3-5). You must be committed and resolved to follow through in obedience to God. The Apostle Paul writes: *…let us not grow weary while doing good, for in due season we shall reap if we do not lose heart* (Galatians 6:9).

    Most failure in life is not a result of true failure; it is simply that we give up. Leadership Coach, Paul Meyer, says, "90% of all those who fail were never actually defeated. They simply quit."

    The process of resolving Marital Debt requires a great deal of courage on the parts of both husband and wife. It will not be easy. However, going through this process will create incredible strength in your relationship that you have probably never had.

A Workable Plan

Ponder the path of your feet, and let all your ways be established. Do not turn to the right or the left; remove your foot from evil (Prov. 4:26-27).

A clear workable plan is necessary to resolving Marital Debt. You will need to have some idea of how you are going to get from where you are to where you need to be.

Your plan needs to be God's plan, because His plan is always better (Isa. 55:8). He has set forth clear principles in His Word that instruct us about relationships and how to navigate them. Below are a few things to consider.

1. *Accountability*: As much as you desire to make significant changes in your life and marriage, your desire alone is not enough. You will need *accountability*. Although accountability may at times come from your spouse, you will also need outside accountability. You will need a personal accountability partner who understands what you have chosen to do and is committed to supporting you. Your spouse will need the same. If these accountability partners happen to be a married couple, you will have the added bonus of this couple providing couple accountability as well.

   Your accountability partner may be a Christian friend. It may be a small group leader, a pastor, or a counselor. Your accountability partner may be anyone of the same gender who is a strong Believer and knows how God's Word applies to real life.

2. *A Proper Apology*: One of the most beneficial tools available to you in resolving Marital Debt is a proper apology. Most of us never learned how to apologize appropriately. Some apologies seem to start out fine, but they end up unclear. Some apologies sound more like excuses to the offender. For example, "I'm sorry *if* I offended you." Or, "I'm sorry, *but* you should not have treated me that way." These so-called apologies are attempted justification for your own inappropriate behavior. Any apology where "but" or "if" is added is in great danger of being an inappropriate apology.

   Dr. Gary and Barbara Rosberg[12] have been speaking and writing on the subject of marriage for many years. One of their staple components is an appropriate apology. They list four components of an apology. These components, adapted from the Rosbergs,[13] can help guide you through the process of communicating clearly with your spouse about the specific debt being addressed.

- *I Was Wrong - Confession*

The first component of an apology is to simply state: *I was wrong.* This is confession of sin (James 5:16). Confessing our sin gives God glory (Joshua 7:19-20). An example can be found in the story of the Prodigal Son (Luke 15). When he realized what he had done and experienced the consequences of his actions, he decided to return home to his father. He composed a speech in which he planned to say to his father, "I have sinned against heaven and before you, and I am no longer worthy to be called your son..." He stated the facts, as he understood them. This statement gives us the standard by which we determine whether our actions are right or wrong—*In God's sight and in your sight.* As the offending party, you may want to defend yourself, but humility requires that you admit to the wrong you have done as God sees it and, in most cases, as your spouse sees it.

Admitting what you have done wrong is the first step toward resolving an issue. *I was wrong for...* (speaking to you in that tone, lying to you about...etc.). You must be specific about what you have done. Do not complicate matters by making vague and unclear statements.

Please note that when you say *I was wrong,* you are not giving your spouse new information. He or she already knows you were wrong! The reason for admitting your wrongdoing is to honor God and take ownership for your actions. You are simply stating the facts.

Also, there is no need, at this point, to explain *why* you did the wrong thing. Your explanation may sound like an attempt to justify your actions. That will make your apology seem insincere.

- *I am Sorry* - Authentic Regret

The next component of a proper apology is *I am sorry.* Note: This must be a true statement. If you are not truly sorry, do not say it. It will only cause problems.

Elaine and I learned the importance of these components when our girls were young. On a particular occasion, a couple of them got into a squabble. One said, "Daddy, she pushed me" (or whatever the offense was). I investigated to find out the details of what happened and said to the guilty party, "Tell your sister you are sorry." She walked over to where her sister was, and with a very unrepentant attitude she said, "I'm sorry!" It was easy to see that she wasn't sorry at all! We realized that we were teaching our children to lie! From that time, we started instructing our girls to say, "I was wrong." That was a fact. Whether she was sorry or not, she needed to admit that what she did was wrong. Of course, we wanted her to be sorry every time. But regardless, the right thing to do was to admit that what she had done was, in fact, wrong.

Being genuinely sorry for what you have done cannot be faked. If it is not real sorrow, the offended party is likely to notice. If you have said "I am sorry" many times to the person you offended, these words may not carry much weight. Usually, the reason is that, although you said you were sorry, you continued to offend in the same way. This makes resolving conflict more difficult, but it is still possible.

Many times, the missing piece which hinders true forgiveness and reconciliation is empathy. To be empathetic means you are able to *understand and share the feelings of another*. When you are able to understand how your actions or words impacted your spouse, he or she will be much more willing to forgive. Your objective is to identify with the injury you have caused.

Let me illustrate. Let's say I borrow your brand new pick-up (a Ford of course). While driving, I decide to send a text message and drive your new pick-up into the side of a building, causing $3000 worth of damage to your vehicle. I come to you and say, "Man, *I am sorry*. I drove your pick-up into a building and damaged the front end. *I was wrong.* I should not have been texting and driving." I may even ask you to forgive me. All this seems fine, except you are probably not listening to what I am saying. Your mind is on your new pick-up! The most important question for you is not whether I am sorry; you are only focused on the damage to your brand new pick-up and who is going to fix it!"

In this scenario, your ability to apologize is overshadowed by the damage done. The same is true in cases when offenses cause deep hurt.

Empathy enables you to understand that your offended spouse is thinking about the damage you caused more than anything else. Your spouse wants to know if you have any clue about how you hurt him or her.

When empathy is absent, a request for forgiveness can seem selfish. It may be perceived that my main objective is to get myself off the hook. We may simply want to move on and forget about the offense. We want our apology to remove any memory from the mind of our offended spouse. This is a self-focused approach to an apology. With this attitude, the chance of the offense being repeated at a later date is very high.

A proper apology communicates to the offended person that you understand how you hurt them—injured them—and what it must have felt like to be hurt by you in that way. If you are not able to connect with the injury, your apology will not likely make a connection with the offended party.

Back to my pick-up illustration. How do we know that I caused $3000 in damages? It is probably because the pick-up was brought to the auto body shop for an estimate. The estimate may come close to the exact amount of the damage. However, the actual cost of repair may be higher or lower once the repair work is done.

Determining the amount of damage done through offenses is not as easy to calculate. Your attempt to understand how you have injured your spouse will cause you to see things from his or her perspective. You can ask the Lord to help you to know how you have hurt her. However, you cannot fully know how she feels without her input. A humble posture will allow you to hear this information and add it to your regret without becoming defensive.

- *I Don't Want to Do that Again* - Repentance

So far, you have admitted that what you did or said was wrong. You have communicated your sincere regret, and now you want to communicate the desire to change. *I don't want to ever do that again.* Another way of communicating this is: *I don't want to be that kind of a person. I don't want that behavior to be a part of my life.*

If you are truly regretful over how you have sinned against your spouse, this statement will be true: The conviction of the Holy Spirit has come, and your humble reception to His correction has caused you to see your sin and its negative impact on others. The natural next step is to ask the Lord to change your heart.

Repentance is a process which starts with a choice. You may not be completely aware of *why* you habitually offend your spouse. As you progress through the process of repentance, you and your spouse will need to work together and allow the grace of God to empower you to do what you cannot do alone. This step does not necessarily guarantee that you will not offend again. You certainly desire to change immediately. However, in real life, ingrained habits create obstacles which make change a growing process.

- *Will You Forgive Me* - Request

The request for forgiveness is one that must be made with the understanding that you, the offender, are in need. You are asking another person (your spouse) to *give you* what you do not have. Only the offended party can give you the gift of forgiveness. Even if God forgives you completely, He cannot give you forgiveness from your spouse. That is a gift only he or she can give.

You will have to ask for it. You cannot demand forgiveness. Forgiveness is not something you deserve. When the forgiveness is given will be on your spouse's timeline. In some cases, a spouse may not be ready to forgive immediately. In such cases, this is between your spouse and the Lord. He or she is human; pain and mistrust are not easy to recover from.

Remember, your motive for apologizing is to please the Lord, not win you your spouse's favor. You may have to simply ask for forgiveness and leave the request with your spouse. This experience is for both of you. God is doing something in you and your spouse through this process. You will both grow in your relationship with the Lord through this process.

The injury you caused may run very deep. A wife may say to her husband, "I want to forgive you, but I just don't think I am at that point today." The offending husband, in this case, will have to respect his wife's response and trust the Lord.

A problem that commonly occurs at this juncture of the process must be avoided. Let's take the case of an offending husband who has humbled himself and has admitted to doing wrong. He has said "I'm sorry" and asked for forgiveness. Yet, when his wife has honest reservations about issuing forgiveness, he may subtly demand it from her. He may think, "Well, Jesus said if you don't forgive me, God's not going to forgive you. You must forgive me!" This reaction reveals a deeply selfish motive. Although what Jesus said is true, this is not the time or the context to bring it up. A comment like this will simply send his wife backward and hinder the entire process. Love is patient and requires that an offending spouse also be patient, as the offended spouse recovers from the offense. It may be that the offended spouse has actually issued forgiveness, but is struggling to trust the offender. It is easy to confuse not forgiving with not trusting. What appears to be unforgiveness, can actually be a hurting spouse trying to recover from a devastating betrayal. The healing process may not take place as quickly as either spouse would like.

Rebuilding Trust

As we have seen, a proper apology includes four components: *I was wrong, I am sorry, I don't want to do that again,* and *will you forgive me?* I want to point out that there is no cookie-cutter approach to forgiveness. Everyone must work through the process of offering forgiveness at their own pace (Phil. 2:12).

In many cases, the consequence of a major offense is *broken trust.* Because trust has been broken, it must be rebuilt. This will take time and consistency.

An illustration may be helpful. Let's compare a healthy connection between a husband and wife as a bridge which crosses a river. The two move freely across this bridge and into each other's life without any reservation. Broken trust is like damaging this bridge that connects you. When trust is broken, it affects everything about your relationship. It changes how you relate and limits the interaction between you. If the broken trust is minor, the damage can be repaired rather quickly and without much inconvenience. It may take only one conversation, issuing a proper apology and for-giveness, to repair it. Other offenses can take longer to repair—a day or longer. After it is repaired, you can get back on the road, so to speak, and everything is back to normal.

If an offense causes severe damage, it can be compared to an explosion causing part of one side of the bridge to collapse. If the explosion takes out one or two lanes, the couple can still navigate around the damage and have some functionality. The repair will take much longer than the minor offense (explained above), but with time, hard work, and consistency, the damage can be repaired. The couple may need addi-tional help to repair the damage.

If, however, the explosion (offense) is such that it takes out the entire side of the bridge, the relationship may come to an abrupt stop. Communication may be little to none. The damage is devastating and the repairs will be costly. It will require major change, and others will certainly need to be called upon for help.

As you assess the items (offenses) in your Marital Debt column, you will need to consider the amount of damage each offense has caused. As I stated earlier, ideally, you will need to practice your debt resolving skills on the smaller debts first.

If you cannot accurately assess the damage from your viewpoint, ask your spouse to help you understand how deeply you have hurt her or him. A sincere request for this information usually has a positive response. However, it must be sincere.

You may not be able to assess by yourself whether your offense toward your spouse was a minor infraction that can be repaired quickly, or a major issue of broken trust. You must get that information from the other person.

Whatever the case, trust usually can be rebuilt. The time it requires will not be wasted. The life-lessons you learn through the process will be very beneficial.

Work on Your Marriage Budget (Individual Worksheet)

Once you have completed the Individual Budget, you and your spouse can compare each budget and work together to come up with your Marriage Budget.

Individual Budget

Personal Debt: Go to your Individual *Marriage Budget Worksheet* (Appendix A) and list any personal debts that you are aware of and have disclosed to your spouse. These are unresolved personal issues that you and spouse are aware of but you have not fully or appropriately addressed. In the right column, list any personal debts that you have not disclosed to your spouse. I suggest listing things that you are unsure about, perhaps a past of present issue that is possibly working against you.

Marriage Debt: Now, list any Marital Debt you think has created barriers between you and your spouse. It doesn't matter who was responsible for the Debt. You are simply listing the items that you believe need to be addressed. Later, when you and your spouse work together on your combined *Marriage Budget Worksheet,* you can discuss the ways these offenses are impacting your relationship. You can find a summary of Common Marital Debts Appendix F.

In the right column, list which debt needs to be addressed first. I suggest starting with the item you believe might be the easiest to address. After you have success resolving the smaller issues, you will be better equipped to address the more delicate ones.

Join the conversation on Facebook. Share how this chapter has been beneficial to you.
https://www.facebook.com/managingyourmarriage

Chapter 6
Investing Through Giving

Marriage Investments are contributions you and your spouse make into others that are intended to propel them toward growth and a lasting marriage.

Marriage Investments are similar to financial investments. Both require intentional forethought, taking risks, and the hope of a future benefit.

To understand investments in the context of marriage, let us consider a few synonyms. To invest means to devote, provide, supply, and entrust. When a couple becomes intentional about making investments into other couples, the process can be very fulfilling.

One difference between financial and marital investments is that marital investments are not intended to benefit the investor (or at least not directly). Jesus explained a principle of God's Kingdom in the Sermon on the Mount. *Do not lay up for yourselves treasures on earth, where moth and rust destroy and where thieves break in and steal; but lay up for yourselves treasures in heaven, where neither moth nor rust destroys and where thieves do not break in and steal. For where your treasure is, there your heart will be also* (Matt. 6:19-21).

The implication here is not to discourage investing. It is to discourage trusting in earthly treasures. Jesus urges His listeners to think and live eternally. We are not to focus only on the temporal and tangible (2 Cor. 4:18). What we treasure must go far beyond ourselves.

According to John 3:16, love involves giving. *For God so loved the world that He gave His only begotten Son, that whoever believes in Him should not perish but have everlasting life.* God so loved...He gave... and in giving, He sought to benefit others.

Marital Investments are intended to benefit others. We see this concept throughout Scripture. One of the cardinal principles of discipleship is to simply share with others what God has shared with you (Matt. 28:20). Jesus said, *Freely you have received, freely give* (Matt. 10:8). The Apostle Paul explained that God comforts us in our trouble, so that we may comfort others (2 Cor. 1:4). Jesus commanded His disciples to ...*love one another as I have loved you...* (John 13:34).

God has designed His Church to care for each other and assist in the growth and development of the Body of Christ (Eph. 4:15-16). Loving your neighbor is a basic tenet of the Christian life.

Every couple has something to invest. Your unique experiences through which you have learned valuable life lessons can be a valuable resource to other couples. There are no experts when it comes to marriage. We are all on the same journey. We have all learned lessons about God, life, our mates, and ourselves.

Jim and Sandy had been through the painful experience of marital betrayal. Jim had cheated on Sandy in the first few years of their marriage. As Jim was seeking to live an authentic life before the Lord, He realized that the Lord wanted him to disclose his unfaithfulness to Sandy. Sandy had no idea. She was devastated. Jim's humble posture and sincere regret helped Sandy move toward forgiveness. The Lord did a beautiful work of healing and restoration in Jim's and Sandy's marriage.

Jim and Sandy were so thankful for how God graciously and gently walked them through the healing process that they wanted to help other couples who were struggling with similar issues. They started by volunteering with a local marriage ministry. They moved chairs, swept floors, and anything else that needed doing. This was their first way of investing in other couples. Eventually, Jim and Sandy opened their home to host a marriage study. They invited friends from work, church, and their neighborhood. At appropriate times, they would tell their story of how God helped them and saved their marriage.

Today, Jim and Sandy are involved in their church's marriage mentoring program and consistently invest in couples. They offered themselves to God in hopes of encouraging couples. They started with what they had. Today, they have an array of resources and experiences to offer couples in need of encouragement.

Although our motive for giving is not to receive, Jesus promised that when we give, God will bless us. *Give, and it will be given to you...* (Luke 6:38). The investments we make into others will certainly bring blessings to us. Every time Jim and Sandy invest in another couple, they strengthen their own marriage.

Ideally, your Income Sources must be adequate enough to provide a surplus. However, even the smallest investment into another couple can benefit them in a huge way. And the investments you make into another couple can easily become an Income Source for your marriage.

You do not need to wait until you have an over-abundance of resources. By simply sharing with others what God has shared with you, you will be participating in the great work of impacting lives.

As with financial investments, Marital Investments require time and consistency if they are going to grow. We must invest *as unto the Lord* (Col. 3:17). Marital Investing is done by faith. We trust that God will take the investments we make into others and use them for His purposes and glory. We may not always see the reward of our investments here on earth (1 Tim. 5:25-26), but we know that we are storing up treasures in heaven. Because Marital Investing is done by faith, there is the tendency to become discouraged if we do not see how our investments are producing a profit. The Apostle Paul's encouragement to the Galatians is appropriate for us as well: *And let us not grow weary while doing good, for in due season we shall reap if we do not lose heart* (Gal. 6:9).

Common Marital Investments

Praying for a couple you know is struggling will help prepare you to look for practical ways to reach out to them.

Marriage Ministry

Those who work in marriage ministry usually focus on one of three general categories: *Prepare, Enrich,* and *Restore.* You and your spouse can get involved in one or more of these areas.

Prepare: Support a Pre-married Couple

More and more couples see the value of good preparation before marriage. Some young couples are actually making premarital counseling part of their wedding plans. Many churches offer pre-marriage classes. These classes are usually led by older couples. Check with your local church to see if there is a pre-marriage program and get involved. If your church does not currently offer pre-married classes, you may be able to help get one started. There are many resources available to choose from.[14]

You may choose to meet with a couple regularly for a few weeks simply to offer support. Most young couples are open to having an older couple in their life. It is not uncommon for these relationships to become long-term friendships, and the younger couple will greatly appreciate the time investment you make.

Our Biblical Counseling Training program can assist those who desire to be better equipped in this area (www.relationalimpact.com).

Enrich: Join couples who want to strengthen their marriages.

There are many great marriage events taking place every year around the Country. Some of these events may be in or near your area. If you're in the San Antonio area, go to http://marriageevents.org hosted by the *San Antonio Marriage Initiative*. Also, http://www.familylife.com/events is a great place to find national events. You can certainly enrich your own marriage by attending an annual marriage event. You can also invest in other couples who cannot afford to attend. Look for a younger couple who could use a weekend away and invest in them by being their sponsor.

Another way you can invest in couples is to offer child-care so they can go on regular dates. You may do this by keeping their children yourself, or you could offer to pay for their childcare so they can have more time together.

Perhaps you can host a small group study on marriage in your home and invite a few younger couples.

Restore: Help Couples in Crisis

Merriam-Webster defines crisis as "a difficult or dangerous situation that needs serious attention." There are several ways you can invest in couples in crisis.

If you already have a relationship with a struggling couple, and they know that you are aware of their situation, you have an opportunity to help them. You may simply suggest that they seek marriage counseling with a Gospel-Centered counselor who can help them from Biblical perspective. See the list of resources in Appendix H.

If your church has a lay counseling ministry, you may suggest the couple call the church to schedule with one of the counselors.

Another way you may invest in a couple's marriage is to offer to pay their way to a weekend intensive. These weekends are usually 2 to 3 days long and focus on the specific needs of the couple.[15]

You may never really know what impact your investment might have in the life of a couple. Jesus said, *when you did it to one of the least of these my brothers and sisters, you were doing it to me!* (Matt. 25:40-NLT)

Get Involved

In summary, here are a few ideas of how you can invest in other couples:

- Invite a couple to your home for a meal and games.
- Host a small group study on marriage. Invite a few younger couples.
- Offer to get involved in pre-marriage education at your church or in your community
- If your church has a marriage ministry, get involved. If it does not, pray about starting one.
- Sponsor (pay for) a couple to attend a marriage seminar. Give the registration to them as a gift (maybe for their anniversary).
- Offer to provide child care for a younger couple so they can have a date night.

You can probably think of other ways to give to other couples. Start today!

Work on Your Marriage Budget (Individual Worksheet)

Turn to your individual *Marriage Budget* worksheet (Appendix A) and list the ways you currently invest in other couples. Then, in the right column, list ideas that you think would be good ways to make investments in couples. Once you have completed the Individual *Marriage Budget,* you and your spouse can compare your ideas and agree on which Investments you will add to your budget.

Join the conversation on Facebook. Share how this chapter has been beneficial to you.
https://www.facebook.com/managingyourmarriage

Chapter 7
Developing a Plan

We have covered the basic components of a *Marriage Budget*. By now, you have completed your Individual *Budget Worksheet*. You (and hopefully your spouse) have listed what you think are Income Sources, Expenses (necessary and unnecessary), Marital Debt, and Investments. Now you and your spouse will need to schedule a time to bring your Individual Budgets together and begin developing your unique *Marriage Budget*.

NOTE: The process of developing your *Marriage Budget* will probably take several conversations. I recommend you schedule a time to cover Income Sources. Some couples will get through this phase faster than others. Don't rush. Take your time and communicate about the items on your lists and why they are important. If you do not finish Income Sources in your first conversation, plan to resume it in the next one. The process of completing your *Marriage Budget* may take several weeks and a few revisions. Your Budget items will probably change through the years, as your circumstances change. An annual review is a good practice to keep your marriage thriving and growing.

Income Sources

Turn to the *Couple Marriage Budget Worksheet* (Appendix B). Compare the items on your *Individual Marriage Budget Worksheets*.

- Are there any items that you both listed in Current Income Sources column? That's great! You agree on these. List these items in the left column of your *Couple Marriage Budget Worksheet*.

- Are there items your spouse did not list? Take time to explain why you listed the items you listed under Current Income Sources. After hearing your spouse share why he or she thinks this item is a Current Income Source, you may agree and list it on your *Couple Worksheet*. Be open to your spouse's ideas and opinions concerning the items listed. If you disagree, ask your spouse if they would be okay placing it in the "Additional Income Sources" column on the right of your *Couple's Worksheet*. If yes, list it in the right column of your *Couple Marriage Budget Worksheet*. If you do not agree on the item, drop it. If it is still important to you later, you can bring it up at a later date.
- After you have each shared your lists of Current Income Sources, dream a little. Think of activities you think *may* be a good Income Source for you as a couple. If you agree that the activity is a possibility, list it in the "Additional Income Source" column on the right side of the *Couple's Budget Worksheet*.
- After you have agreed on the items in the Income Source category, Current and Additional, get your calendar and schedule when and where you plan to begin incorporating your Income Sources. Like all budgets, you may find that it is necessary to make adjustments along the way. That is totally okay. Some Income Sources are good for a particular season of life. A new season may require changes. Grow and change with these seasons.

Congratulations! You have done a lot of work to get to this point. But you are not yet finished. This process is not merely academic. In other words, it is not enough to get your Income Sources listed on your *Marriage Budget* and calendar. You must follow through and schedule the activities you have listed. This is where you start developing growth habits so you can have consistent Marital Income in your marriage.

Expenses

- Turn to the *Couple Marriage Budget Worksheet* (Appendix B) and compare the items on your *Individual Marriage Budget Worksheets*. Are there any items that you both listed in the Expense category?
- Next, share with each other the Expense items that you listed on your *Individual Worksheet*. If you both listed the same items, great! You agree. Simply list these items on your *Couple's Worksheet*. If your spouse listed items you didn't, discuss these. Allow each one to share why he or she listed these

items as a Necessary Expense. Be open to your spouse's ideas and opinions concerning the items you listed.

- If you listed additional Necessary Expenses in the right column of your *Individual Worksheet*, share with your spouse why you think this Expense needs to be added.

- After comparing your *Individual Marriage Budget Worksheets*, list the items you agree on in your *Couple Marriage Budget Worksheet*. If you disagree on items, you may want to discuss these. If an agreement is not reached, drop the issue for now. You may come back to it at a later time.

Unnecessary Expenses

Follow the same pattern as you did for Income Sources and Necessary Expenses. When you are finished comparing your lists of items, follow the instructions above so that you have an agreed upon list on your *Couple Marriage Budget Worksheet*.

This category is where you may begin to touch sensitive issues. Some of the items on your lists may point to offensive behavior and things that are simply unnecessary for your relationship. Be careful! You may be tempted to become defensive when you see what your spouse listed as *Unnecessary* on his or her *Individual Worksheet*. Be open to seeing things from your spouse's perspective. God may use the information to show you things you have not have seen about yourself. We all have blind spots when it comes to our interaction with others.

As you go through these Unnecessary Expenses, you may need to go through the process of issuing a proper apology (see chapter 6). Remember the story of the Prodigal Son (Luke 15). He realized he had sinned in both God's and his father's eyes. Restoration for these offenses will require humility and openness.

Ideally, you will want to develop a short-term plan for changing the behaviors you have apologized for. If you need help developing this plan, ask someone you know who has successfully changed their habits. They will be happy to assist you. You may also contact our office for help in finding a Biblical counselor to assist you (www.relationalimpact.com).

Take a few moments to pray together about your relationship. You may ask, "Lord, these are the things we know we need to change in our marriage. Will You help us?" Discuss practical ways you can implement new changes. God's Word is full of examples of putting off old sinful behavior and replacing these with new ways that are Christ-like (Eph. 4:20-32; Rom. 12:1-2; Col. 3:7-9).

Marital Debt

Follow the same procedure for this category as you did for the others, comparing the items you each listed. Then list the items you agree on in your *Couple's Worksheet*.

It takes courage and an honest look at yourself to successfully work through this category. If you find that you and your spouse disagree on these items, at least communicate about them. Many times a person's heart will grow calloused and closed when they have been hurt. Remember, broken trust and deep wounds cannot be healed and repaired quickly. It requires time, consistency, and a genuine desire to please the Lord and be obedient to Him.

You may remember things you did in the past to hurt your spouse but have never have apologized for. This is a good time to do so. Go through the four components of an apology (Chapter 6). Work through these debts as best you can. Start with the smallest debt. Focus on one issue at a time. You may only be able to focus on one issue during one conversation. That's fine. You will have other times to work on your *Marriage Budget*. This is an ongoing project that will require effort but will produce a lot of profit. You will need to ask for and issue forgiveness. By doing this, you will hit the restart button on your relationship. The sooner you pay off a Marital Debt, the sooner you free up marital resources and the better you will connect with your spouse and grow toward oneness.

Don't get discouraged if you spend days, weeks, or months working through a deep hurt. The process will yield great rewards for you and your relationship. If you get stuck in the process, you may need to find some help from a pastor or a counselor. That is okay. You will be all the wiser for asking for help.

Investments

Follow the procedure of the above categories. Compare your *Individual Marriage Budget Worksheet* items from the Investment category. List the Investments you agree on in your *Couple Marriage Budget Worksheet*. You may already have items that you placed in your *Current Investments* column.

An investment is something you do together to invest in other couples and/or your future.

Like Income Sources, Investments require intentional effort and planning. Get your calendar and schedule when and where you plan to begin incorporating a new Investment. Agree on a specific couple you want to invest in. Write down their names and contact information. Schedule a time this week to contact them and get together. As a couple, come up with ideas. Ask what you can do to invest in other couples. You will find a few suggestions in chapter 7. Commit to act on one of your items in the next few weeks.

By the time you have completed your *Marriage Budget Worksheet,* you will have:

- Increased your marital Income by adding new Income Sources
- Reduced your Unnecessary Expenses by communicating and agreeing on what to get rid of
- Started working on resolving your Marital Debt—resolving conflict
- Started investing in your marriage and in other couples

Congratulations! You have now begun the process of approaching your marriage relationship in a comprehensive manner. Marriage Management involves commitment, resolve, endurance, a plan, assistance, prayer, teamwork, good communication skills, willingness to change, and an ever increasing desire to please the Lord. I believe the Lord will bless you in ways you may have never imagined.

In the seventh chapter of the book of Matthew, Jesus told a story of two men who set out to build a house (also translated family). One was a wise man and the other was a foolish man. Both built their houses. Both encountered the same obstacles. But the wise man's house stood firm through the storm because he built his house on the rock. *He who hears these sayings of mine and does them, I will liken him unto a wise man who builds his house upon the rock...beat on that house, but it did not fall because it was founded on a rock.* Matthew 7:24-27. By putting into practice what Jesus taught, you will be building your marriage and family on a sure foundation.

Chapter 8
Final Words
(about Managing Your Marriage)

The Necessity of Work

Good marriages don't just happen. They require hard work, understanding, perseverance, commitment, and other elements. The simple example of an ant conveys this principle:

Take a lesson from the ant, you lazy bones. Learn from their ways and become wise. Though they have no prince or governor or ruler to make them work, they labor hard all summer, gathering food for the winter, but you, lazy bones, how long will you sleep? When will you wake up? A little extra sleep, a little more slumber, a little folding of the hands to rest. Then, poverty will pounce on you like a bandit. Scarcity will attack you like an armed robber. (Proverbs 6:6-11 – NLT).

The lesson is clear: ants are self-motivated. They do what is necessary for success. They instinctively know they must store up food so that, when winter comes, they will have resources to survive. The ant plans ahead because his survival depends upon it.

How does this passage apply to marriage? If you and your spouse want a life-long and fulfilling marriage, it will require hard work and initiative.

God Blesses Hard Work

Opportunity is missed by most people because it is dressed in overalls and looks like work.

- Thomas Edison

The ant is one example of how hard work yields benefits and success. Other passages highlight the blessings that come from working hard.

He who has a slack hand becomes poor, but the hand of the diligent makes rich (Proverbs 10:4).

The soul of a lazy man desires, and has nothing; but the soul of the diligent shall be made rich (Proverbs 13:4).

The lazy man will not plow because of winter; he will beg during harvest and have nothing (Proverbs 20:4).

James writes of the practical missing element of work when he addresses the expectations of those who wanted God's blessings.

...be doers of the word, and not hearers only, deceiving yourselves. For if anyone is a hearer of the word and not a doer, he is like a man observing his natural face in a mirror; for he observes himself, goes away, and immediately forgets what kind of man he was. But he who looks into the perfect law of liberty and continues in it, and is not a forgetful hearer but a doer of the work, this one will be blessed in what he does (James 1:22-25).

...this one will be blessed in what he does! As in the story of the two builders (Matthew 7), we find the secret to God's blessings: obedience—doing what He instructs. Although prayer is needful and beneficial, prayer alone will not save or build your marriage. Saving your marriage will require *doing* what God's Word instructs.

Your Marriage on Paper

Couples who struggle because of low or limited Marital Income usually are focused on their Expense and Debt categories. They pray about what they *don't have* and think about how they wish the negative stuff was gone. For example, a couple asks God to remove their conflicts. When He doesn't respond like they expect, they can easily become disgruntled with God. They figure that if God would remove the problems (expenses and debt) from their marriage, they would be fine. The struggling marriage is not God's fault. He will not remove from your marriage the things He will use to grow you.

Marital Debt and Unnecessary Expenses are certainly problems which need attention, but the couple also needs more Marital Income. In the Marriage Budget, focusing on Income Sources will positively impact your negative categories (Unnecessary Expenses and Debt).

At the end of the day, marriage requires Management. If a couple learns to manage their marriage, they will be able to find contentment in whatever circumstances they find themselves.

Limited Tolerance for Error

Mary turned to John with tears and asked, "How did we get here?" I have seen this scenario played out many times. It is the question two well-meaning individuals ask themselves when their relationship hits the brick wall and confusion sets in. Most couples really want to make their marriage work. They want to be life-long companions. Their intentions are good. But, when a relationship is neglected and important issues are ignored, a couple finds themselves in a place they never thought they would be.

Here is how we get to that place. When a couple is newly married, they have a good bit of emotional resources and a large amount of tolerance in their relationship. When the wife offends her husband, he may choose to ignore the offense and not talk about it. He reasons, "Why bring it up? Why rock the boat?". The offended party, in effect, absorbs the offense and chooses to move on in the relationship with seemingly no consequence. However, as a result, the couple's emotional resources decrease. Little by little, one offense after another begins to deplete their resources and their tolerance for error becomes less and less. Eventually their emotional capacity is emptied and their tolerance for error ends. Now, even the smallest offense becomes the proverbial straw that breaks the camel's back. One day, she says, "I've had enough! I'm done! I can't take this anymore!". The perplexing thoughts of the offender are: "I've done that 100 times! Why are you reacting like this now?". The answer is simple. Every previous offense which was not addressed appropriately took positive resources from the relationship. In every case, not dealing with the issue properly depleted their marital resources. Although these neglected offenses were costly, the couple was unaware that these offenses were slowly weakening their relationship.

In the above example, the couple did not have adequate Income Sources to replace what these offenses were costing them. Eventually, they were on the verge of losing their marriage because of poor management.

The Marriage Covenant Belongs to God

Just a couple more points, and then we're done. It is important to understand that, from a Biblical perspective, your marriage is not yours. It belongs to God! He created it. He owns it! I like to think of it in the context of a songwriter. If I write a song today, the song legally and immediately becomes mine. I am the owner. No one can record the song without my permission. Otherwise, he is breaking the law. If I allow someone to use my song for a recording, I will benefit from the usage (in the way of royalties).

The relationship between God and the marriage covenant is very similar. God allows us to enter into His marriage institution. We are not to enter it lightly. It is a life-long covenant. We are not allowed to do with it whatever we please, including dissolving it. Jesus warned, *what God has joined together, let not man separate.* (Matthew 19:6). The implication is: God is involved in the making of your marriage covenant and should be consulted about its usage. If the marriage covenant belongs to God, then that makes us stewards. And, as stewards, we must assume certain responsibilities and seek to please God by our management (stewardship) of His covenant. In turn, He receives honor (royalties, if you will).

Marriage Doesn't Do Anything

It is important to understand that a marriage does not do anything! You cannot fix a marriage. You cannot make a marriage better. This may sound odd coming from a Biblical counselor who specializes in marriage counseling. My point is simple. A marriage reflects the condition of the two individuals in it. If the individuals in the marriage are strong, growing, and healthy, they will likely have a strong, growing and healthy marriage. If they are two struggling individuals, they will have a struggling marriage. Strong people = strong marriages. Struggling people = struggling marriages. Your marriage reflects you and your spouse. If you want a better marriage, you must commit yourself to the growth process. Personal growth is one of the secrets to a happy marriage.

 Join the conversation on Facebook. Share how this book has been beneficial to you.
https://www.facebook.com/managingyourmarriage

Chapter 9
Group Discussion Questions

CHAPTER ONE
Discussion Questions

1. Chapter mentioned three connecting points for couples. 1. Relational/emotional 2. Physical and 3. Spiritual. On which points do you and your spouse connect the most?

2. What did you get out of chapter one?

3. How might seeing your marriage through the lens of a budget practically help you?

4. When you think of Income Sources for your marriage, upon which do you and your spouse agree?

CHAPTER TWO
Discussion Questions

1. Do you and your spouse agree on which items are Necessary Expenses? If not, which do you disagree on?

2. Each couple has unique marital expenses, depending on circumstances, season of life, etc. What are the two most demanding things that directly require your marital resources?

    1. _____
    2. _____

3. Can you identify the signs of not having enough emotional resources? I.e. How does your lack of emotional capacity to appropriately manage these demands show up?

4. How might viewing these demands through the Marriage Budget help you anticipate your needs and thus help you manage your marriage better?

CHAPTER THREE
Discussion Questions

1. Were you able to identify any Unnecessary Expenses that you personally contribute to your marriage?

2. In what ways do you think removing Unnecessary Expenses would improve your marriage?

3. It is much easier to see fault in others than in ourselves. This can cause us to justify our bad choices. Take a minute and consider how you and your spouse may be feeding one another's bad choices.

4. What is one thing you can do to minimize pushing your spouse's buttons?

CHAPTER FOUR
Discussion Questions

1. Were you able to identify any Unnecessary Expenses that you personally contribute to your marriage?

2. In what ways do you think removing Unnecessary Expenses would improve your marriage?

3. It is much easier to see fault in others than in ourselves. This can cause us to justify our bad choices. Take a minute and consider how you and your spouse may be feeding one another's bad choices.

4. What is one thing you can do to minimize pushing your spouse's buttons?

CHAPTER FIVE
Discussion Questions

1. Personal debt affects a marriage. Is there anything from your past that you have not acknowledged and received forgiveness for?

2. Imagine you and your spouse resolving past conflicts. How would this enrich your relationship?

3. How might seeing your marriage through the lens of a budget practically help you?

4. Issuing an apology and forgiveness is vital to moving past relational debt. What steps could you take to move toward you spouse?

CHAPTER SIX
Discussion Questions

1. Can you think of a couple who invested in your marriage? If yes, share what that meant to you.

2. Can you think of a couple you can invest in? What might your investment look like?

3. How might you be part of encouraging couples in your church, neighborhood, or community?

4. Does your church have a ministry to marriages? If not, how might you help start one?

CHAPTER SEVEN
Discussion Questions

1. If you are going through this book as a small group, bring your budget to your next gathering and share with the group what your budget looks like.

2. Could you benefit from another couple being your accountability partners? Who might you ask to walk beside you in your marriage journey?

3. What has been the most beneficial part of going through this book?

4. How has your relationship changed since you began using the Marriage Budget?

Join the conversation on Facebook. Share how this chapter has been beneficial to you.
https://www.facebook.com/managingyourmarriage

Appendix A

Marriage Budget Worksheet (Individual Use)

Income Sources: Current

_____

_____

_____

_____

_____

Income Sources: Additional (New)

_____

_____

_____

_____

_____

Necessary Expenses: Current

_____

_____

_____

_____

_____

Necessary Expenses:Additional (New)

_____

_____

_____

_____

_____

Unnecessary Expenses (Known to your spouse):

_____

_____

_____

_____

_____

Unnecessary Expenses (List in order of priority):

1. _____

2. _____

3. _____

4. _____

5. _____

Marriage Debt (offenses that have occurred in your marriage):

_____

_____

_____

_____

_____

Marriage Debt (To be addressed in priority):

1. _____

2. _____

3. _____

4. _____

5. _____

Investments and Giving: Current

_____

_____

_____

_____

Investments and Giving: Additional (New)

_____

_____

_____

_____

Download free Marriage Budget Worksheets at www.relationalimpact.com

Appendix B

Marriage Budget Worksheet (Couple Use)

Income Sources: Current

_____
_____
_____
_____
_____

Income Sources: Additional (New)

_____
_____
_____
_____
_____

Necessary Expenses: Current

_____
_____
_____
_____
_____

Necessary Expenses: Additional (New)

_____
_____
_____
_____
_____

Unnecessary Expenses:

_____
_____
_____
_____

Unnecessary Expenses (List in order of priority):

1. _____
2. _____
3. _____
4. _____
5. _____

Marriage Debt (Agreed upon):

_____
_____
_____
_____

Marriage Debt (Address Smallest to largest):

1. _____
2. _____
3. _____
4. _____
5. _____

Investments and Giving: Current

_____
_____
_____
_____

Investments and Giving: Additional (New)

_____
_____
_____
_____

Appendix C

Summary of Income Sources

(Deut. 25:4; Pr. 10:4-5; 12:21; 13:23; 27:23; 28:19;2 Thess. 3:10; 1 Tim. 5:8)

- Prayer
- Life-Long Commitment (Gen. 2:24; Matt. 19:6; Gal. 6:9;   Heb. 10:36)
    - Believing that Divorce is not an option
    - Being Committed to being the best you can be
    - Understanding that your marriage is a *marathon*, not a sprint
    - Maintaining Mutual Trust and Honesty (the foundation of trust, vulnerability)
    - Doing the things that build trust (trust is sometimes in the debt category)
- Good Communication (includes:
    - Speaking truthfully (Eph. 4:15)
    - Sharing your thoughts, opinions, facts, etc.
    - Conflict Resolution skills (Problem Solving)
    - Good Listening skills (Jam. 1:19)
    - Non-verbal communication (Sowing affection, A smile, a wink,)
- Mutual Respect -
    - Giving honor (Rom. 12:10; Phil. 2:3; 1 Pet. 3:7)
    - Being Courteous
    - Showing Kindness (1 Cor. 13:4; Gal. 6:1; Eph. 4:32)
    - Being Thoughtful and considerate
    - Appreciating Differences
    - Accepting one another unconditionally
    - Viewing your spouse as a gift from God

- Realistic Expectations (Ps. 62:5; Ps. 118:8; Jn. 2:24-25)
  - Knowing the limits of marriage and what to expect
  - Problems are common to every relationship
  - Growth and change come slowly
  - Your spouse is human just like you
- Practicing Forgiveness (Matt. 6:14; Mk. 11:25; Eph. 4:32; Col. 3:12-13; Eccl. 7:21-22)
  - Keeping short accounts
  - Being Gracious
  - Showing Mercy
  - Realizing that you are married to a sinner
  - A great book is *"When Sinners Say I Do"* by Dave Harvey
- Being Friends (Gen. 26:8; Pr. 5:18; 17:17; 18:24)
  - Enjoying Companionship
  - Sharing life together—the journey
- Having Fun Together (shared activities - Pr. 5:18; Mal. 2:14)
  - Regular Dates
- Enjoying Friends Together (Social income sources-
  (Rom. 14:19; Col. 3:16; Heb. 10:24; 1 Jn. 4:7-8)
- Romantic Enjoyment (Pr. 5:15-18; Song of Sol. 3:4-5; 8:3-4)
  - Non sexual fondness – wooing each other
  - Enjoying and appreciating the beauty of your sexual relationship
  - Giving one another special attention
- Spiritual Intimacy
  - Praying together (1 Pet. 3:7; Matt. 18:19; Acts 1:14)
  - Worshiping together (Ps. 122:1 – *I was glad when they said...*)
  - Learning together (like this Marriage Seminar)
  - Serving Together
- Maintaining Teamwork (Rom. 12:18; 14:18; Phil. 2:13)
  (Mal. 2:14-15; Rom. 12:16; 1 Cor. 1:10)
  - Working toward your dreams and common goals
  - Compromising personal interest for the benefit of the marriage
  - Considering your spouse as better than yourself (Phil. 2:3)
  - Parenting as a team
  - Sharing family responsibilities

Appendix D
Summary of Necessary Expenses

- Learn good communication skills
- Financial issues
- Parenting issues (unity)
  - Pregnancy, new baby, teenage years
- Praying together
- Regular dates
- Resolving conflict
- Unexpected challenges
- Emotional struggles

  May be due to:
  - Illness
  - Infertility
  - Dealing with loss (job, loved one)
  - Illness or emotional issues may require. These may require personal sacrifices (sexual, schedule, etc.)
- Decision making
- Aging parents

Appendix E
Summary of Unnecessary Expenses

- Busy schedules (overly committed)
- Unnecessary arguments
- Criticism
- Contempt
- Defensiveness
- Stonewalling
- Apathy
- Selfishness
- Selfish demands
- Disrespect
- Sinful angry
- Dishonesty (keeping secrets)
- Bad habits (especially if they've been brought to your attention)
- Conflict over parenting Issues
- Flirting
- Spending too much time away from Home
- Personal weakness
- Controlling
- In-Law interference
- Financial irresponsibility
- Unrealistic expectations
- Misunderstanding conflict
- Bitterness and resentment

Appendix F
Summary of Marital Debt

Marital Debt comes in all shapes and sizes. A huge debt for one couple may be a minor debt for another. The list below is designed to simply get you headed in the right direction as you consider which relational debts you and your spouse have. Remember, items in the Unnecessary Expense list can become Marital Debts if they are not addressed.

Broken Trust through:

- Lying
- Infidelity (affairs: physical and emotional)
- Sexual Offenses (Pornography, selfish demands)
- Financial Irresponsibility (over spending, not paying bills)
- Abuse (physical, verbal, emotional, sexual)
- Indifference (apathy, passivity)
- Chronic Bad Habits
- Others not listed here

Appendix G
Summary of Martial Investments

- Marriage Ministry
    - *Prepare*
    - *Enrich*
    - *Restore*
- Prepare: Support a Pre-married Couple
- Enrich: Join couples who want to strengthen their marriages.
- Restore: Help Couples in Crisis
- Get Involved
    - Invite a couple to your home for a meal and games.
    - Host a small group study on marriage. Invite a few younger couples.
    - Offer to get involved in pre-marriage education at your church or in your community
    - If your church has a marriage ministry, get involved. If it does not, pray about starting one.
    - Sponsor (pay for) a couple to attend a marriage seminar. Give the registration to them as a gift (maybe for their anniversary).
    - Offer to provide child care for a younger couple so they can have a date night.

Appendix H
Resources

The Relational Impact Group	http://relationalimpact.com
San Antonio Marriage Initiative	http://samarriage.com
Growing Love Network	http://www.growinglovenetwork.org/love-reboot
Breakthrough Moments	http://www.growinglovenetwork.org/love-reboot
Be Broken Ministries	http://2.bebroken.com
Reengage	http://marriagehelp.org
The Austin Stone Counseling Center	http://www.austinstonecounseling.org
The Third Option	http://www.thethirdoption.com
Retrouvaille	http://www.retrouvaille.org/

END NOTES

1. Shaunti Feldhahn, *The Good News About Marriage: Debunking Discouraging Myths About Marriage and Divorce* Multnomah, 2014

2. Timothy Keller and Kathy Keller, *The Meaning of Marriage: Facing the Complexities of Commitment with the Wisdom of God*, Riverhead, 2013

3. https://www.census.gov/prod/2005pubs/p70-97.pdf

4. Stormie Omartian, *The Power of a Praying Wife*, Harvest House Publishers 2014; Stormie Omartian, *The Power of a Praying Husband*, Harvest House Publishers 2014; Stormie Omartian, *A Book of Prayers for Couples*, Harvest House Publishers 2011

5. Dr. Emerson Eggerichs, *Love & Respect: The Love She Most Desires, the Respect He Desperately Needs*, Thomas Nelson 2004; Dr. Les Parrott and Dr. Leslie Parrott, *Saving Your Marriage Before It Starts* Zondervan 2015; Gary Chapman, *The 5 Love Languages: The Secret to Love That Lasts*, New Edition, Northfield Publishing 2015; Joseph M. Stowell, *The Weight of Your Words*, Moody Publishers 1998; Dr. Gary Rosberg, Barbara Rosberg, *6 Secrets to a Lasting Love: Recapturing Your Dream Marriage*, Tyndale House 2007

6. Ed Wheat and Gaye Wheat, *Intended for Pleasure*, Fourth Edition Revell 2010; Dr. Gary Rosberg, Barbara Rosberg and Ginger Kolbaba, *The 5 Sex Needs of Men & Women: Discover the Secrets of Great Sex in a Godly Marriage*, Tyndale House / 2007; Dr. Kevin Leman, *Sheet Music*, Tyndale House 2003

7. The Relational Impact Group, www.relationalimpact.com

8. http://.familylife.com, http://datenightnorthtexas.com, https://woodhills.org/product-category/free-downloads,

9. Does Divorce Make People Happy? *Findings from a Study of Unhappy Marriages, http://www.lifeissues.net/writers/edi/edi_03divorcemarriage.html*

10. http://www.merriam-webster.com/dictionary/resentment

11. Tammy Nelson, Ph. D, http://www.huffingtonpost.com/2013/08/12/emotional-affair_n_3722057.html

12. Dr. Gary Rosberg, Barbara Rosberg, *6 Secrets to a Lasting Love: Recapturing Your Dream Marriage*, Tyndale House 2007

13. Dr. Gary Rosberg, Barbara Rosberg, *6 Secrets to a Lasting Love: Recapturing Your Dream Marriage*, Tyndale House 2007

14. Find great resources at the San Antonio Marriage Initiative website: http://samarriage.com/marriage-preparation-resources.htm

15. http://samarriage.com/marriage-intensives.htm

www.relationalimpact.com